PREWRATH

A VERY SHORT INTRODUCTION

ALAN E. KURSCHNER
Author of *Antichrist Before the Day of the Lord*

PREWRATH

A VERY SHORT INTRODUCTION

TO THE GREAT TRIBULATION, RAPTURE, AND DAY OF THE LORD

ESCHATOS PUBLISHING

Copyright © 2014 by Alan E. Kurschner

All rights reserved. No part of this publication may be reproduced, stored in a retrieval system, or transmitted in any form or by any means—for example, electronic, photocopy, recording—without the prior written permission of the publisher. The only exception is brief quotations in printed reviews.

Eschatos Publishing
P.O. Box 107
Pompton Lakes, NJ 07442

Printed in the United States of America

Publisher's Cataloging-in-Publication

Kurschner, Alan.
Prewrath : a very short introduction to the great tribulation, rapture, and day of the Lord / by Alan Kurschner.
pages cm
Includes bibliographical references and index.
LCCN 2014935834
ISBN 978-0-9853633-2-1

1. End of the world. 2. Second Advent.
3. Antichrist. I. Title.

BT877.K87 2014 236'.9
QBI14-600058

Unless otherwise noted, all Scripture is from the New English Translation (NET) of the Bible, copyright 1996–2014. Unless otherwise noted, all Greek definitions are from *A Greek-English Lexicon of the New Testament and Other Early Christian Literature*, rev. and ed. Fredrick W. Danker, 3rd ed. (Chicago: University of Chicago Press, 2000).

Jacket Design: Teddi Black
Interior: Linda M. Au

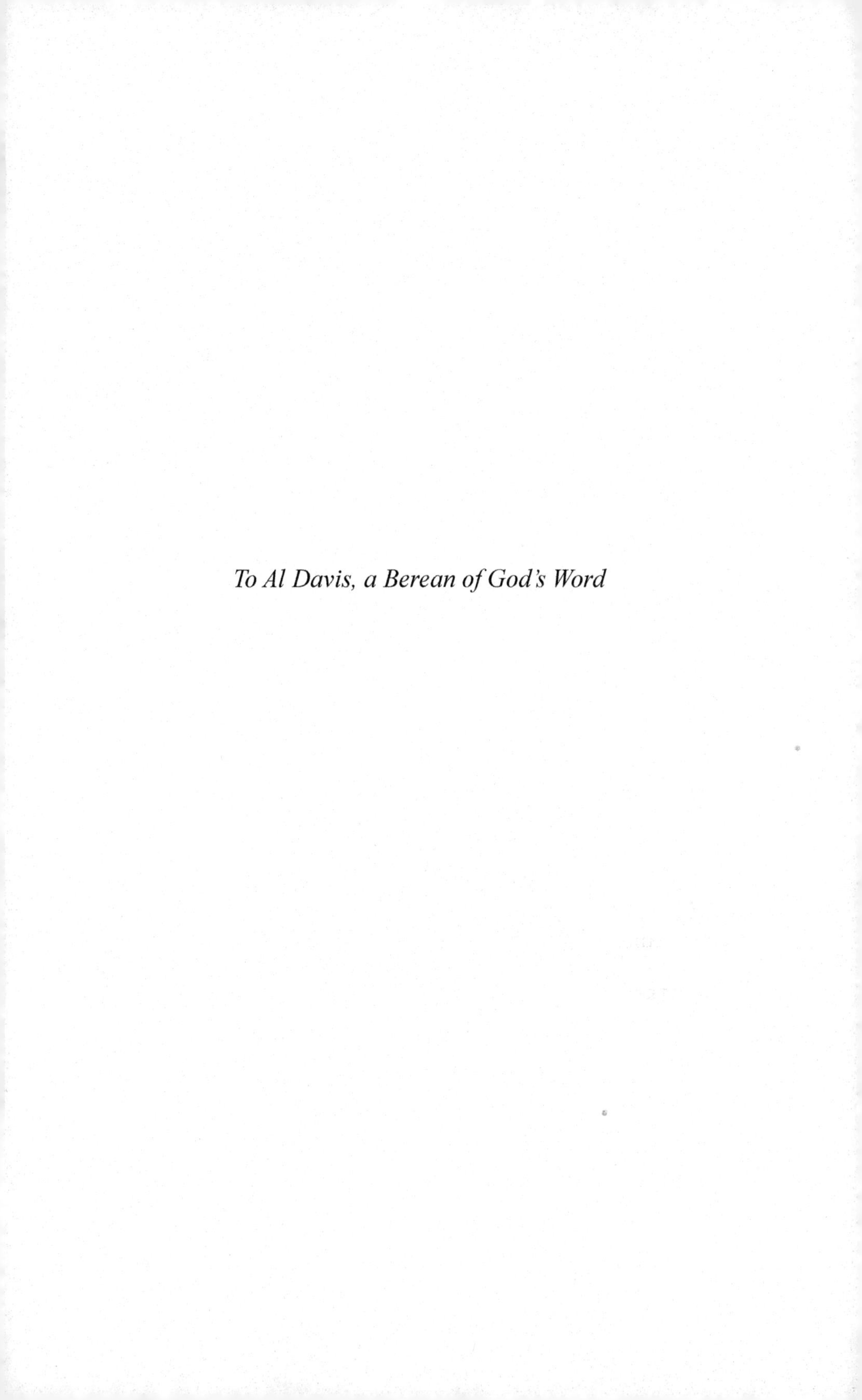

To Al Davis, a Berean of God's Word

Contents

Illustrations

Figures

Tables

Introduction

P*rewrath: A Very Short Introduction to the Great Tribulation, Rapture, and Day of the Lord* is an excerpt from my book *Antichrist Before the Day of the Lord: What Every Christian Needs to Know About the Return of Christ* (Pompton Lakes, NJ: Eschatos Publishing, 2013). This excerpt is a bare-bones introduction to the prewrath interpretation of the second coming of Christ, while *Antichrist Before the Day of the Lord* puts flesh on those bones. Even though I highly encourage reading the latter book for a full-orbed description, I recognize there are some who desire a quicker read to get an overview before reading further. I have also written this excerpt with the hope that this short book would be widely distributed. I believe this message is urgent and it is my desire to see as many Christians as possible be introduced to its biblical message.

This book is about the second coming of Christ. It is part of the larger Christian teaching called "eschatology," which comes from the Greek word *eschatos* ("last"), meaning "the study of last things." My goal is to focus on what the biblical writers believed were the most prominent issues related to the second coming. What are these issues and where can they be found in the Bible?

Let me take the last question first. In the Old Testament, the relevant endtime issues are found mostly in the writings of the prophets. In the New Testament, they are found in Jesus' Olivet Discourse (Matthew 24–25; Luke 21; Mark 13), Paul's teaching in the Thessalonian epistles, and, not surprisingly, the book of Revelation. Thus, these are the biblical passages I will be drawing from.

Next, what are the major issues related to the return of Christ in these passages? In this book, I will be writing from what is called the "prewrath" perspective. The prewrath position places importance on three central events related to Christ's return: (1) the Antichrist's great tribulation, which will happen just before Christ's return; (2) the rapture of God's people, which will happen on the first day of Christ's return; and (3) the day of the Lord's wrath, which will begin immediately after the rapture. These three events will be treated in the three parts of this book.

Some may question why a book on Christ's return is necessary. They may say, "What only matters is that Jesus is returning!" This sounds pious, but it is not biblical. What this implies is that these other "side" issues regarding the great tribulation, the rapture, and the day of the Lord's wrath were not concerns for the biblical writers. It may come as a surprise, however, that the biblical writers themselves did not believe that it was sufficient simply to know that Christ is returning. Indeed, Jesus *is* coming back, and there is no question that knowing this truth should propel us to holy living. But Jesus himself ominously warns us to be aware of what will happen *before* he returns: "See, I have told you beforehand" (Matt. 24:25). Jesus, Paul, and the book of Revelation consistently teach that the church will have her faith tested by the Antichrist and his persecution during the great tribulation. In the context of describing this persecution, Jesus asks, "When the Son of Man comes, will he find faith on earth?" (Luke 18:8). Paul commands, "Let no one deceive you in any way" (2 Thess. 2:3). The book of Revelation warns, "This requires the steadfast endurance of the saints—those who obey God's commandments and hold to their faith in Jesus" (Rev. 14:12). It is imperative, then, that every believer take this seriously.

The endtime teachings of Jesus (Matthew 24–25), Paul (1 and 2 Thessalonians), and the book of Revelation give prominence to the event of the Antichrist's great tribulation that will happen before Jesus returns for his church. In fact, in the Olivet Discourse, Jesus places more emphasis on how to live during the testing period before his return than on his return itself! Accordingly, we, too, must model Jesus' example by emphasizing the ramifications of the Antichrist's great tribulation upon the church. The task for the student of prophecy is to affirm not just *that* Jesus is returning but the *conditions* surrounding his return. This includes the Antichrist's persecution, the period when God will refine his bride for his Son's arrival.

This prewrath teaching may sound new—even challenging—to some. You might have grown up in a tradition that believed we will be raptured before the Antichrist's great tribulation (as I did). If this describes you, I encourage you to be a "Berean" in the faith and test everything in this book against the Word of God. "These [Bereans] were more open-minded than those in Thessalonica, for they eagerly received the message, examining the scriptures carefully every day to see if these things were so" (Acts 17:11).

Four Major Outlooks on Biblical Prophecy

Before we begin our study, let's look at four interpretations of the endtimes to provide a broader understanding of the discussion.

The first outlook, or approach, is futurism. Futurists interpret most of the events in the Olivet Discourse, 1, 2 Thessalonians, and the book of Revelation as yet to be fulfilled. For example, futurists believe that the Antichrist and his great tribulation are still to come, an event that will occur just before Christ comes back, and not an event that has already been fulfilled or that is being fulfilled at the present time. The second outlook is preterism, which believes that these events, including the Antichrist's great tribulation, have already been fulfilled. Preterism holds that these events were fulfilled in the first century in relation to the destruction of Jerusalem in A.D. 70. The third outlook is historicism, which interprets events such as the Antichrist's great tribulation as being fulfilled throughout the church age between the first and second comings of Christ (also called "interadvental"). The fourth outlook is idealism, which interprets these events only as symbolic or spiritual—as timeless ethical truths about the struggle between good and evil.

In this book, my approach is futurist, so I will be writing primarily for those who share this outlook. This is not to say that preterists, historicists, and idealists cannot benefit from this book, because some of their concerns will overlap at points with futurism.

Four Major Futurist Positions

Within futurism, there are four primary futurist positions—pretribulationism, midtribulationism, posttribulationism, and prewrath. One characteristic that makes these positions futurist is they affirm that there will be a future seven-year period during which the three major endtime events unfold. I will say more on this seven-year period in Part 1. All these positions also affirm that believers are promised exemption from the day of the Lord's wrath. "For God did not destine us for wrath but for gaining salvation through our Lord Jesus Christ" (1 Thess. 5:9). Accordingly, an important question for all of these positions is, When does the day of the Lord's wrath begin in relation to the seven-year period? The correct answer to this question will inform us of when the rapture takes place in relation to the seven-year period. I will briefly outline the main tenets of each of the futurist positions.

Pretribulationism teaches that the seven-year period, which pretribulationists refer to as "the tribulation," is entirely the day of the Lord's wrath. Thus, they see the rapture as occurring just before the seven-year period begins. According to pretribulationism, the church will not face the Antichrist's great tribulation since the rapture will happen first. Pretribulationism does not make a distinction between the Antichrist's great tribulation and the day of the Lord's wrath.

PRETRIBULATIONAL MODEL

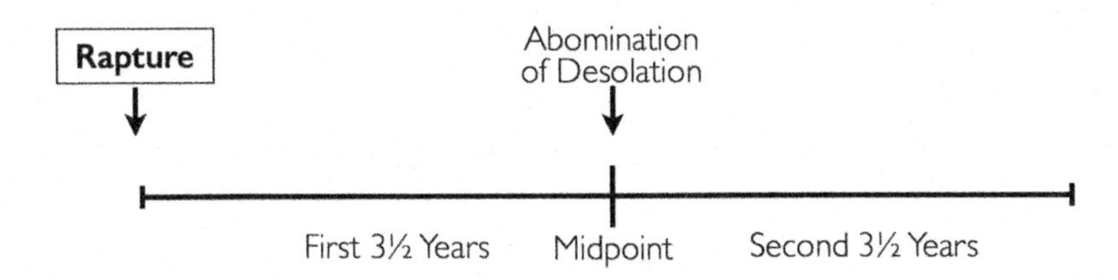

(The Day of the Lord covers the entire seven years
i.e. the "Tribulation Period")

Midtribulationism has variants to its position, but at its core, it teaches that the rapture will happen at the midpoint of the seven-year period before the Antichrist's great tribulation. This position shares affinity with pretribulationism in that it views the rapture as happening before the Antichrist's great tribulation. In recent decades, the midtribulational position has become practically defunct. I am mentioning it here for completeness' sake.

MIDTRIBULATIONAL MODEL

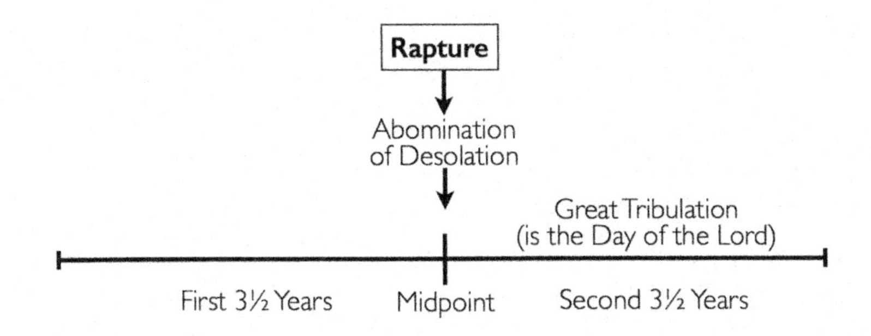

Posttribulationism teaches that the rapture will happen at the completion of the seven-year period. Some posttribulationists deny a future seven-year period, yet they still affirm that the major prophetic events will happen in the future. Unlike pretribulationism and midtribulationism, this view believes that the church will face the Antichrist's great tribulation. It holds that the day of the Lord's wrath occurs within a single twenty-four-hour day at the very end of the seven-year period. (Some posttribulationists have the day of the Lord's wrath unfolding during the second three-and-one-half years as God physically protects the church on *earth* while he pours out his wrath upon the ungodly.)

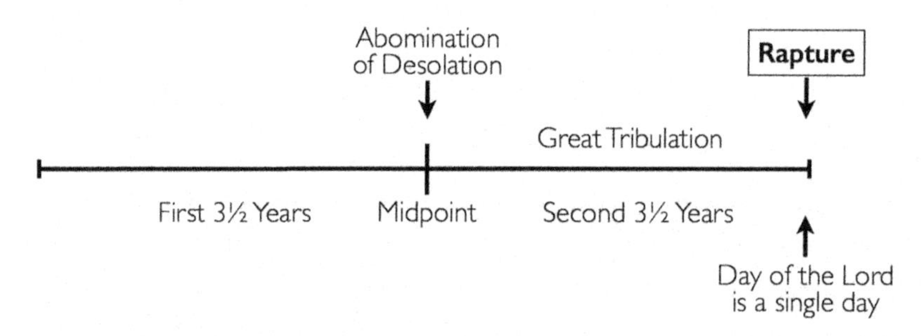

Prewrath teaches that the rapture will occur sometime during the second half of the seven-year period. We do not know the exact day or hour (Matt. 24:36). Prewrath makes an important biblical distinction between the events of the Antichrist's great tribulation and the day of the Lord's wrath. The Antichrist's great tribulation will be directed against the church, and at some unknown time, those days will be cut short with the coming of Jesus to resurrect and rapture God's people. Then God will immediately begin to pour out his day-of-the-Lord wrath against the ungodly.

PREWRATH MODEL

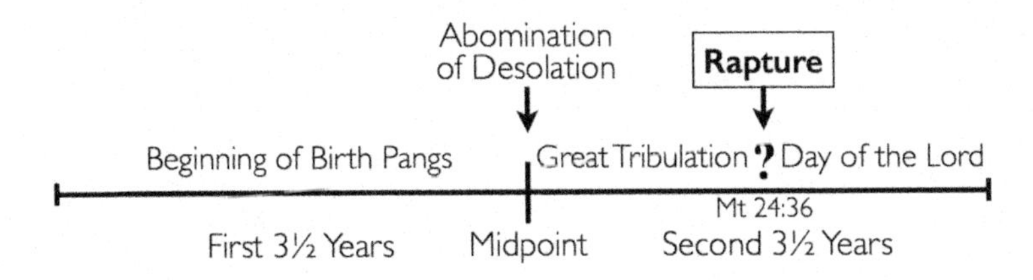

? = The question mark means that Christ's return to resurrect and rapture God's people will happen at an unknown day and hour (Matt 24:36). But it will occur sometime during the second half of the seven-year period. When the rapture occurs on that unknown day, it will cut short the Antichrist's great tribulation against believers followed by the day of the Lord's wrath against unbelievers.

Many of us were taught that the church will be "raptured out of here" *before* the Antichrist's persecution. However, I will show that the Bible consistently instructs us that the church will first experience the Antichrist's great tribulation before Christ returns to rapture his people and execute his wrath upon his enemies—hence "prewrath."

PART 1.
The Antichrist's Great Tribulation

I have entitled Part 1 "The Antichrist's Great Tribulation" to highlight that this period is characterized by the Antichrist's persecution against God's people. It is not the period of God's wrath. The Antichrist's fury will be against the church, as well as a remnant of Jews who will not capitulate to him. We will learn that the Bible makes an important distinction between the period of the Antichrist's great tribulation and the day of the Lord's wrath. The great tribulation will happen first, and it will be followed by God's judgment. In Part 1, I will describe the nature and purpose of the Antichrist's great tribulation, drawing from Jesus' Olivet Discourse, Paul's Thessalonian epistles, and concluding with the book of Revelation.

Seven-Year Time Frame

The Bible teaches that a future seven-year period represents the final seven years of this age. Pretribulational teachers mistakenly equate this period with what they have coined as "the tribulation period." This expression is misleading because it is vague and, as we will learn, neglects the biblical distinction between the great tribulation and the day of the Lord. Therefore, I will refer to this period using the neutral term "the seven-year period."

Why did God ordain this time frame? In Daniel 9, the prophet Daniel anguished over the sins of rebellious Israel and prayed to God, confessing on behalf of his nation and asking for mercy, forgiveness, and repentance. While Daniel was praying, God sent a prophetic word through the angel Gabriel. Daniel was told that God would take a block of 490 years out from history to accomplish the following: "Seventy weeks [i.e. 490 years] have been determined concerning your people and your holy city to put an end to rebellion, to bring sin to completion, to atone for iniquity, to bring in perpetual righteousness, to seal up the prophetic vision, and to anoint a most holy place" (Dan. 9:24). In the generations subsequent to Daniel, the first 483 years of the 490 were fulfilled by the time of the first century; however, the last seven years remain to be fulfilled. At the conclusion of this period, the prophecy of Israel's salvation will be accomplished.

Since I am assuming a futurist approach in this book, I will not take the time here to argue for the futurity of the seven-year period.[1] However, I want to make several comments on this temporal framework. A very important verse is Daniel 9:27:

> He [the Antichrist] will confirm a covenant with many [Israel] for one week [i.e. seven years]. But in the middle of that week he will bring sacrifices and offerings to a halt. On the wing of abominations will come one who destroys, until the decreed end is poured out on the one who destroys. (cf. Dan. 12:11)

This verse states "he" will confirm a covenant with many for "one week" (*šāḇûa*), which in this Hebrew context denotes seven years. The New English Translation rendering "confirm" may not capture the force of the underlying Hebrew verb *gābar*. The English Standard Version renders it "make a strong covenant," which better captures the sense; but the sense behind the Hebrew may better indicate oppressing, imposing, or coercing, suggesting that the other party to the covenant may not have much say in the matter.[2] The "he" is an antichrist figure. The covenant may be for protection or permission to reinstitute the sacrificial system in return for some other service or action. It is implied that the Antichrist will break the covenant by stopping the sacrifices and offerings, causing abominations. This will occur in the middle of that week (i.e. the midpoint of the seven-year period). Accordingly, the "many" refers to Israel since the covenant relates to the stopping of the sacrifices and offerings associated with the Jewish temple. However, the "many" could also suggest that most of Israel will support the covenant, but a remnant will dissent.

A question remains, Will we recognize the signing of the covenant when it happens and thereby know that we have entered the seven-year period? I do not think we can be certain that we will. What will be unmistakable, however, is the midpoint event—the revelation of the Antichrist and his abomination of desolation. We will see that Jesus, Paul, and the book of Revelation never focus on the beginning of the seven-year period, let alone mention the signing of a covenant. The absence of this event in key New Testament passages suggests that the writers did not consider it important enough to focus our attention on it. Instead, all three New Testament sources stress that it is at the midpoint at which there will be the discernible event by which believers will know for certain that they have entered the season of the great tribulation.

ANTICHRIST'S SEVEN-YEAR COVENANT

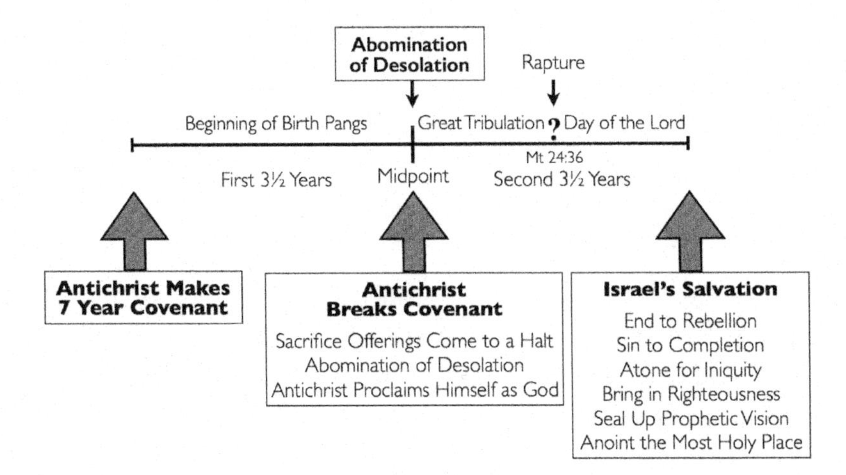

Having established a seven-year timeline, we can situate key prophetic events beginning at the midpoint, including when the Antichrist will commit abominations and stop sacrifices and offerings. I will consider the nature and purpose of the Antichrist's persecution program called the great tribulation, drawing from Jesus' Olivet Discourse, followed by Paul's teaching, and concluding with the book of Revelation.

Situating Jesus' Olivet Discourse

The Olivet Discourse given on the Mount of Olives was one of Jesus' last instructions to his disciples before he was crucified. The Olivet Discourse is recorded in the three synoptic gospels (Matthew 24–25, Mark 13, Luke 21). I have chosen Matthew's account since it is the fullest of all three, and I will draw from Luke's and Mark's accounts when helpful. There are seven sections to Matthew's account. In Part 1, I will cover through the great tribulation up to verse 28.

Outline of Matthew 24–25	
24:1–3	Prediction of the Temple
24:4–8	The Beginning of Birth Pangs
24:9–14	The Great Tribulation
24:15–28	The Great Tribulation Developed
24:29–31	The Day of the Lord Begins
24:32–25:30	Similes and Parables for Watchfulness
25:31–46	Sheep and Goats Judgment

Matthew 21 records the so-called "triumphal entry," which eventually ends in conflict between Jesus and the Scribes and Pharisees, who repeatedly challenged his authority. This culminates in Jesus pronouncing seven woes against these hypocrites, followed by his lament of the obstinate and unrepentant hearts of the Jewish leadership. Matthew 24 begins with Jesus walking away from the temple after this confrontation with the Jewish leaders, causing his disciples confusion and distress. Attempting to salvage something from the conflict, the disciples draw Jesus' attention to the splendid temple structures as if to reconcile him back to the laurels of Israel's religious achievements. But Jesus would not be taken in by such externalities. Matthew records,

> Now as Jesus was going out of the temple courts and walking away, his disciples came to show him the temple buildings. And he said to them, "Do you see all these things? I tell you the truth, not one stone will be left on another. All will be torn down!" (Matt. 24:1–2)

Jesus had previously prophesied the destruction of Jerusalem (Luke 19:41–44). But now he completes this prediction by focusing on the epicenter of life in the city, the temple. The fulfillment of these two prophecies occurred a few decades later in A.D. 70 when the Romans razed Jerusalem and the temple was destroyed.

In Matthew 23:39, Jesus told the Jewish leaders he was leaving them. "For I tell you, you will not see me from now until you say, 'Blessed is the one who comes in the name of the Lord!'" This announcement and Jesus' prediction of the temple's destruction prompted the disciples to ask two questions: "Tell us, when will these things happen?" and "What will be the sign of your coming [*parousia*] and of the end of the age?" (Matt. 24:3). The Greek noun for "coming" is *parousia,* which means "an arrival and a continuing presence."[3] It is the term behind the expression "second coming" or "second advent." The Lord's second coming (*parousia*) will be a comprehensive-complex whole. In other words, it will not be a simple, brief event as the rapture will be. Instead it will span various events that will fulfill divine purposes.

We can illustrate this by looking at Jesus' first coming. When we think of this event, we do not think exclusively of his birth. His birth was his arrival, but his subsequent presence included his upbringing, teaching ministry, miracles, discipling, death, burial, and resurrection. It was a complex whole that God used to fulfill his purposes. Similarly, the second coming will begin with Jesus' arrival in the clouds to resurrect the dead and rapture them along with believers who are alive at that time (1 Thess. 4:13–18). The biblical writers often emphasized the arrival aspect of the parousia because they wanted to induce godly living in their listeners. But it would be a mistake to think they viewed it as limited only to Jesus' glorious appearing in the sky to resurrect the dead and rapture all believers. This is because his subsequent presence will encompass major events such as the day of the Lord's wrath, bringing the remnant of Israel to salvation, and reclaiming his earthly regal-rule, which will extend into the millennium. In short, Christ is coming back as deliverer, judge, and king.

The Beginning of Birth Pangs

The disciples' questions imply that they assumed that the destruction of the temple buildings and the consummation of the age would be a twofold event with both events happening about the same time. However, Jesus will challenge this preconceived notion as well as other kingdom categories. During Jesus' ministry, whenever he was asked a direct question it was common for him to ignore the question, reply with a question, or give an unexpected answer to the question that challenged the preconceived beliefs. In this case, he chooses the latter, taking the opportunity to challenge the disciples' preconceived eschatological categories, especially about the kingdom of God. Jesus will teach them that deceptive temptation and great suffering must come first for those who desire to be in his kingdom at the consummation. The disciples' question elicits from Jesus one of his longest recorded teachings in the gospels, the Olivet Discourse. He opens:

> "Watch out that no one misleads you. For many will come in my name, saying, 'I am the Christ,' and they will mislead many.

> You will hear of wars and rumors of wars. Make sure that you are not alarmed, for this must happen, but the end is still to come. For nation will rise up in arms against nation, and kingdom against kingdom. And there will be famines and earthquakes in various places. All these things are the beginning of birth pains." (Matt. 24:4–8)

Before Jesus reveals the sign of his return (vv. 27, 30), he describes a cluster of conditions that must happen first. He cautions the disciples not to be alarmed when these things happen, thinking wrongly that the end of the age is imminent because it will first be a time of tumult in the world (politically and naturally), as well as for the church (false messiahs and false teachings). To describe this period, Jesus uses the metaphor "beginning of birth pangs." This period will be characterized by hardship; otherwise, his warning not to be misled or alarmed would not be meaningful. The period will not be as intense as the labor pains during the great tribulation, which Jesus says will be an unprecedented time for God's people. Nevertheless, the beginning of birth pangs will be an intensely challenging time for the church, both physically and spiritually.

THE BEGINNING OF BIRTH PANGS

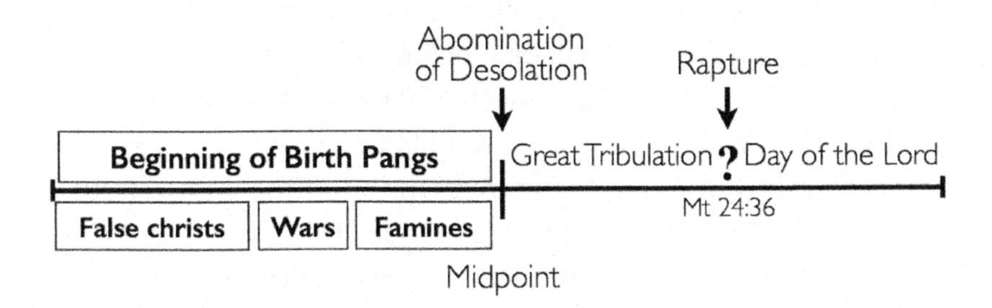

The Great Tribulation

We have seen that Jesus taught that the beginning of birth pangs is preliminary to his return, but he warned that the events that comprise it should not be mistaken to signal the arrival of the end. Now his teaching shifts to the heightened persecution of believers, the period we know as the great tribulation.

> "Then they will hand you over to be persecuted [*thlipsis*] and will kill you. You will be hated by all the nations because of my name. Then many will be led into sin, and they will betray one another and hate one another. And many false prophets will appear and deceive many, and because lawlessness will increase so much, the love of many will grow cold. But the person who endures to the end will be saved. And this gospel of the kingdom will be preached throughout the whole inhabited earth as a testimony to all the nations, and then the end will come." (Matt. 24:9–14)

This section takes the birthing imagery to its next stage, the great tribulation. Believers will face a cluster of trials and temptations that Jesus summarizes as martyrdom, hatred, apostasy, betrayal, deception, and lawlessness. In the next section, starting at verse 15, we will see that Jesus relates back to verses 9–14, developing the great tribulation by describing how and when martyrdom will be brought about. But at this point (vv. 9–14), Jesus warns of the future onset of persecution and martyrdom. This warning extends to the church at large since the disciples are representatives of the church: "You will be hated by all the nations because of my name." Believers are persecuted and put to death because of Jesus' name, for his name represents the gospel, a gospel the world hates. Even today, the mere mention of the name "Jesus" is met with animosity in public discourse. This will reach a crescendo just before Christ returns, expressed through universal persecution and martyrdom.

Next, we are told "many will be led into sin, and they will betray one another and hate one another." These three acts will likely be committed by the same persons. The expression "led into sin" refers to apostasy (cf. Mark 4:17; 14:27, 29). The pressure of persecution will be too much for them, showing them to be only professors of the faith, not true believers. To avoid persecution, many rationalizations and creative pretexts will be given. Yet they will not be content with their apostasy for they will betray and hate one another (cf. Mark 13:12).

Jesus also prophesies that many false prophets will appear and deceive many (cf. vv. 4–5). It is likely that those who apostatize will fall prey to these false prophets. In addition, Jesus says the love of many will grow cold because of a surge in lawlessness. This "many" in verse 12 may be referring to the "many" in verse 11 who will be led into sin or apostasy. Verse 12 also states, "lawlessness will increase so much." Literally, it can read, "lawlessness being made complete," which implies a climax of lawlessness. In the parable of the wheat and weeds, Jesus says those who commit lawlessness at the end of the age will be destroyed. "So just as the tares are gathered up and burned with fire, so shall it be at the end of the age. The Son of Man will send forth His angels, and they will gather out of His kingdom all stumbling blocks, and those who commit lawlessness" (Matt. 13:40–41 NASB).

Paul uses the same term for "lawlessness" (*anomia*) to refer to the climax or completion of lawlessness embodied in the Antichrist. "Let no one deceive you in any way. For that day will not come, unless the rebellion comes first, and the man of lawlessness is revealed, the son of destruction" (2 Thess. 2:3 ESV). Paul connects the man of lawlessness with the rebellion. Some translations render "rebellion" as "apostasy," since the Greek term behind it is *apostasia*. Later, we will have more to say on Paul's teaching on this point. In short, Jesus and Paul are indicating that the cause of the eschatological apostasy is related to the fulfillment of lawlessness.

In verse 13, Jesus promises, "But the person who endures to the end will be saved" (cf. v. 14). In this context, he is not speaking of spiritual salvation but physical deliverance. Those who survive to the end will be delivered, as we will learn, through the rapture when the parousia begins (Matt. 24:31; cf. 1 Thess. 4:17).

The Great Tribulation Developed

> "So when you see the abomination of desolation—spoken about by Daniel the prophet—standing in the holy place (let the reader understand), then those in Judea must flee to the mountains. The one on the roof must not come down to take anything out of his house, and the one in the field must not turn back to get his cloak. Woe to those who are pregnant and to those who are nursing their babies in those days! Pray that your flight may not be in winter or on a Sabbath. For then there will be great suffering [i.e. tribulation] unlike anything that has happened from the beginning of the world until now, or ever will happen. And if those days had not been cut short, no one would be saved. But for the sake of the elect those days will be cut short. Then if anyone says to you, 'Look, here is the Christ!' or 'There he is!' do not believe him. For false messiahs and false prophets will appear and perform great signs and wonders to deceive, if possible, even the elect. Remember, I have told you ahead of time. So then, if someone says to you, 'Look, he is in the wilderness,' do not go out, or 'Look, he is in the inner rooms,' do not believe him. For just like the lightning comes from the east and flashes to the west, so the coming of the Son of Man will be. Wherever the corpse is, there the vultures will gather." (Matt. 24:15–28)

Verse 15 is one of the most important structural verses in the Olivet Discourse. It introduces a parenthetical section clarifying and unpacking the previous section: "So when you see the abomination of desolation—spoken about by Daniel the prophet—standing in the holy place." In other words, verses 15–28 do not sequentially follow verses 9–14; instead, they thematically *develop* verses 9–14 on the tribulation, persecution, and spiritual action the believer is to take. We know this to be the case for a few reasons. Most importantly, verse 15 begins with the conjunction "so" (*oun*), which some Bible versions render "therefore." This conjunction functions inferentially as a "deduction, conclusion, or summary to the preceding discussion."[4] A second reason for the parenthetical nature is that the audience in verses 15–28 is the same as the audience before verse 15. Jesus uses the second person "you" consistently without any hint that he has two different groups of believers in view. The same "you" in verse 9 is the same "you" in verse 15 (see also vv. 20–26). There is a final reason for the parenthetical nature in verses 15–28. While verses 9–14 give a general or "shotgun" description of events that will precede the end of the age, verses 15–28 draw attention to the spiritual response of the believer who will experience the events.

THE GREAT TRIBULATION

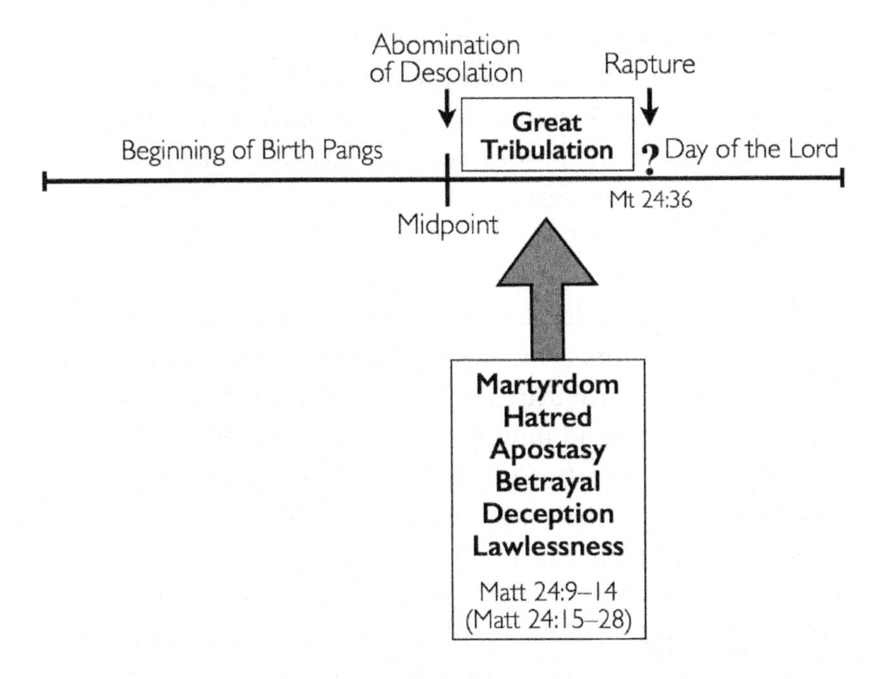

Jesus uses the expression "the abomination of desolation" to portray a personification of the Antichrist: "So when you see the abomination of desolation—spoken about by Daniel the prophet—standing in the holy place" (Matt. 24:15). Drawing from the prophet Daniel, Jesus uses this expression to personify the Antichrist as a detestable idol that causes sacrilege (Dan. 9:27, 12:11).

We should recall that, with Jesus referring to this verse, he is establishing a point of reference at the midpoint of the seven-year period (cf. Dan 9:27).

As noted above, the apostle Paul gives this desolating Antichrist figure the epithet "man of lawlessness" (2 Thess. 2:3–4; see also Dan. 7:25; 11:36). And the book of Revelation uses the imagery "beast," developing more on his desolating actions.

> One of the beast's heads appeared to have been killed, but the lethal wound had been healed. And the whole world followed the beast in amazement; they worshiped the dragon because he had given ruling authority to the beast, and they worshiped the beast too, saying: "Who is like the beast?" and "Who is able to make war against him?" The beast was given a mouth speaking proud words and blasphemies, and he was permitted to exercise ruling authority for forty-two months. So the beast opened his mouth to blaspheme against God—to blaspheme both his name and his dwelling place, that is, those who dwell in heaven. (Rev. 13:3–6)

In light of these desolating actions, we understand why Jesus says this will initiate an unequaled time of persecution. "For then there will be great tribulation, such as has not been from the beginning of the world until now, no, and never will be" (Matt. 24:21 ESV). The Greek word for "tribulation" is *thlipsis,* which denotes one or more of the following experiences: tribulation, pressure, affliction, trouble, suffering, and persecution. It should be noted that this term can be applied to describe a woman's birth pangs (e.g. John 16:21). Previously, Jesus spoke of the "beginning of birth pangs" (v. 8), but now the birthing stage is intensified to "great [*megas*] tribulation."

In our eschatological context in Matthew 24, the Antichrist's great tribulation will be directed against—not the ungodly—but believers (v. 22). Revelation consistently echoes Jesus' teaching concerning this brutal period.

> The beast was permitted to go to war against the saints and conquer them. He was given ruling authority over every tribe, people, language, and nation, and all those who live on the earth will worship the beast, everyone whose name has not been written since the foundation of the world in the book of life belonging to the Lamb who was killed. If anyone has an ear, he had better listen! If anyone is meant for captivity, into captivity he will go. If anyone is to be killed by the sword, then by the sword he must be killed. This requires steadfast endurance and faith from the saints. (Rev. 13:7–10)

So great will this martyrdom be that Jesus says, "If those days had not been cut short, no one would be saved [i.e. delivered]. But for the sake of the elect those days will be cut short" (Matt. 24:22). In the same vein, Paul says God's people in the midst of eschatological persecution will be given "rest" when the Lord returns. "[A]nd to you who are being afflicted to give rest together with us when the Lord Jesus is revealed from heaven with his mighty angels" (2 Thess. 1:7). It is no wonder that the fifth seal martyrs cry out to God, "How long, Sovereign Master, holy and true, before you judge those who live on the earth and avenge our blood?" (Rev. 6:10).

Persecution, however, will not be the only adversity for God's people during the great tribulation. It will be compounded by deceptive temptation to capitulate to false teachings.

Deception during the Great Tribulation

False messiahs and prophets will use deceptive signs and wonders to try to convince people to follow them. But Jesus exhorts,

> "Then if anyone says to you, 'Look, here is the Christ!' or 'There he is!' do not believe him. For false messiahs and false prophets will appear and perform great signs and wonders to deceive, if possible, even the elect. Remember, I have told you ahead of time. So then, if someone says to you, 'Look, he is

> in the wilderness,' do not go out, or 'Look, he is in the inner rooms,' do not believe him." (Matt. 24:23–26)

The rise of these false christs and false prophets will not be a phenomenon to take lightly. Jesus prophesies that they will use persuasion ("do not believe him") and deceit ("I have told you ahead of time"). This will be so great a temptation that, according to Jesus, if it were possible to deceive even the elect, it would happen. The temptation against God's people will be real and strong. The fact that they are believers (the elect) does not excuse them from their human responsibility to resist and stay faithful. Through these warnings, God will work his persevering grace to protect them from apostasy (cf. Phil. 1:6; 1 Thess. 5:23–24; 1 Cor. 10:13; John 6:39; John 10:28–29; 1 Pet. 1:5–6).

Paul on the Apostasy and the Revelation of Antichrist

In his second epistle to the Thessalonians, the apostle Paul links false teaching and apostasy to the revelation of the Antichrist. Since Paul's instruction on this subject is one of the most important in the Bible, we will devote adequate space to it.

> Now concerning the coming of our Lord Jesus Christ and our being gathered together to him, we ask you, brothers, not to be quickly shaken in mind or alarmed, either by a spirit or a spoken word, or a letter seeming to be from us, to the effect that the day of the Lord has come. Let no one deceive you in any way. For that day will not come, unless the rebellion comes first, and the man of lawlessness is revealed, the son of destruction, who opposes and exalts himself against every so-called god or object of worship, so that he takes his seat in the temple of God, proclaiming himself to be God. Do you not remember that when I was still with you I told you these things? And you know what is restraining him now so that he may be revealed in his time. For the mystery of lawlessness is already at work. Only he who now restrains it will do so until

> he is out of the way. And then the lawless one will be revealed, whom the Lord Jesus will kill with the breath of his mouth and bring to nothing by the appearance of his coming. The coming of the lawless one is by the activity of Satan with all power and false signs and wonders, and with all wicked deception for those who are perishing, because they refused to love the truth and so be saved. (2 Thess. 2:1–10 ESV)

In 2 Thessalonians 1, Paul encouraged the Thessalonian believers to persevere in adversity, reassuring them that these tribulations are not the eschatological day of the Lord's judgment and that God will deliver his people unto rest and glorification at Christ's revelation. Continuing this topic of the day of the Lord into 2 Thessalonians 2, Paul gives additional reassurance to the Thessalonians that they are not experiencing the day of the Lord's wrath. He will do this by describing two prophesied events that must happen before the day of the Lord. In chapter 1, Paul stressed that the day of the Lord *will come*; in chapter 2, he will stress that the day of the Lord *has not come*.

Beginning in verse 1, Paul writes,

> Now regarding the arrival of our Lord Jesus Christ and our being gathered to be with him. (2 Thess. 2:1)

He links two events with each other: "the arrival of our Lord Jesus Christ" and "our being gathered." The term for "arrival" is *parousia*. Some other translations render this as "coming," but the rendering "arrival" emphasizes the starting point for the parousia, and by extension, it carries the notion of an ongoing presence. The expression "our being gathered" (*episynagōgē*) recalls Paul's previous teaching on the rapture (1 Thess. 4:15–18; cf. 2 Thess. 1:7). More on this latter point in Part 2.

THE PAROUSIA AND THE GATHERING

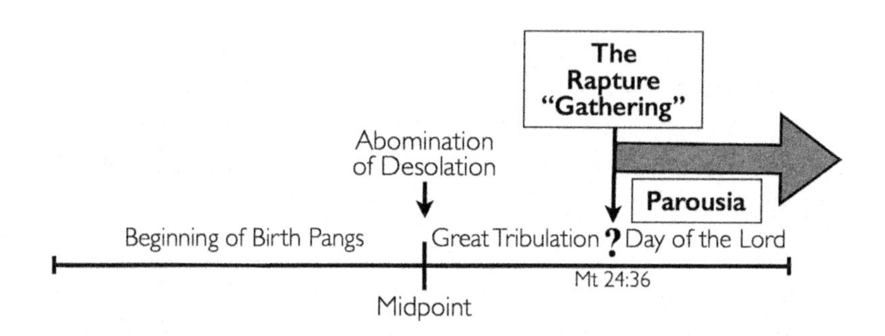

Next, Paul exhorts,

> [We ask you, brothers and sisters,] not to be easily shaken from your composure or disturbed by any kind of spirit or message or letter allegedly from us, to the effect that the day of the Lord is already here. (2 Thess. 2:2)

In this verse, Paul describes the aforementioned gathering and parousia as "the day of the Lord." It was brought to Paul's attention that the Thessalonians had come to erroneously believe that the day of the Lord had already commenced. This jolts Paul into pleading with them not to be "easily shaken from your composure or disturbed." The false teachers in Thessalonica did not deny a day of the Lord—they affirmed it. Their error was teaching that it was happening already. Since Paul had previously taught that the Thessalonians would be delivered from the Lord's wrath (1 Thess. 5:9), we can imagine their frightened state of mind thinking they had been left for judgment. Paul must combat this false teaching immediately.

The mistaken eschatology by the Thessalonian believers in 2 Thessalonians 2:2 was anticipated by Paul in 2 Thessalonians 1:5–10, where he laid a foundation of hope, teaching that they would be delivered at the revelation of Christ before the day of the Lord's judgment. In short, since the revelation of Christ had not occurred, the Thessalonians can be certain that the day of the Lord's wrath had not arrived either. Paul then provides additional certitude of this truth by explaining that two events must happen first.

> Let no one deceive you in any way. For that day will not come, unless the rebellion comes first, and the man of lawlessness is revealed, the son of destruction, who opposes and exalts himself against every so-called god or object of worship, so that he takes his seat in the temple of God, proclaiming himself to be God. (2 Thess. 2:3–4 ESV)

Paul begins by using strong language, warning the Thessalonians not to be deceived or misled through any manner. The reason why they—and by extension all Christians—should not be deceived is because the day of the Lord will not happen until two events happen first: (1) the rebellion comes, and (2) the man of lawlessness is revealed. Some have misunderstood this to mean that the rebellion will be the first event and the revelation of the man of lawlessness will be the second. But Paul does not make this sequential argument. He lumps these two related events together, instructing that both must occur before the day of the Lord. The context will give us clues to the relationship between the rebellion and the revelation of the Antichrist.

Without elaborating on its precise nature, Paul simply states that "the rebellion" (*ho apostasia*) must come. Other translations, which I prefer, render it as "the apostasy," a term better capturing the nuance. The Greek term means a "defiance of established system or authority, rebellion, abandonment, breach of faith." This can be abandonment of either political or religious convictions. In our context, it indicates the latter, religious apostasy. But what sort of religious apostasy does Paul have in mind? It is most likely an apostasy of the eschatological *professing* church. In the Greek, it is significant that there is an article before "apostasy" because it points to a discernible event.[5] It will be a significant apostasy happening with the professing church during the Antichrist's coming, a separating out of unbelievers from the remnant of believers in the church.

There are two reasons I believe this to be the correct interpretation. First, in our context, *apostasia* is associated with an eschatological, Satan-inspired rejection of the truth, especially seen in verses 9–12 (cf. 1 Tim. 4:1; Matt. 24:9–13, 23–26). In the immediate context, we find a cluster of expressions of the Christian faith and truth from which Paul exhorts the Thessalonians not to depart:

- "not to be easily shaken from your composure or disturbed" (v. 2)
- "Let no one deceive you in any way" (v. 3)
- "they found no place in their hearts for the truth" (v. 10)
- "Consequently God sends on them a deluding influence" (v. 11)
- "through sanctification by the Spirit and faith in the truth" (v. 13)
- "stand firm and hold on to the traditions that we taught you" (v. 15)

The second reason why the apostasy will be the eschatological professing church relates to the prophesied event that must occur before the day of the Lord, the Antichrist's revelation (*apokalyptō*, which means "to cause something to be fully known, reveal, disclose, bring to light, make fully known"). Paul associates the Satan-inspired apostasy with the revelation of the Antichrist. In turn, he associates the Antichrist's revelation with the time he "opposes and exalts himself above every so-called god or object of worship, and as a result he takes his seat in God's temple, *displaying himself as God*" (2 Thess. 2:4, emphasis mine). Since the Antichrist will demand that the world worship him, his demand establishes an unambiguous test for those who claim to be Christians: the choice to apostatize or stay faithful. The Antichrist will become the "object of worship," with false-professing Christians apostatizing their empty faith. In short, the apostasy will be devilish, discernible, deceptive, and damning.

Paul uses the epithet "the man of lawlessness [*anomia*]" to describe the Antichrist, because he will oppose God's law. So much so, he "opposes and exalts himself above every so-called god or object of worship." The Antichrist will not just be *a* man of lawlessness but *the* man of lawlessness, making him the ultimate embodiment of lawlessness in human history. To be sure, there is a "hidden power" of lawlessness already at work at this time (cf. 2 Thess. 2:7), but it will one day manifest into a physical, literal individual. Paul then piles on another epithet for the Antichrist: "the son of destruction," which means he is destined for destruction (cf. v. 8; Rev. 17:8, 11).

Paul associates the Antichrist's revelation with him taking "his seat in God's temple, displaying himself as God." Thus, a temple will have to be rebuilt if he is to take his seat there. To be sure, the temple that will be rebuilt before the midpoint of the seven-year period will not be divinely sanctioned, for it will be part of an attempt to reinstate the old Mosaic system. Presumably, the rebuilding will be spearheaded by Orthodox Jews seeking to reestablish a holy place for Levitical sacrifices and other temple rituals prescribed in the Torah.[6]

THE MIDPOINT EVENTS OF THE SEVEN-YEAR PERIOD

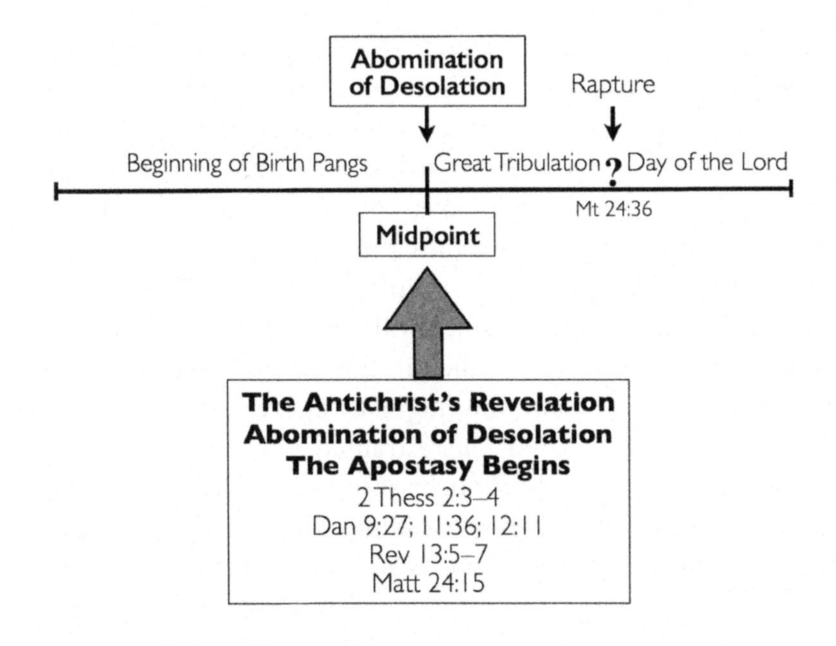

The Restrainer

> And so you know what holds him back, so that he will be revealed in his own time. For the hidden power of lawlessness is already at work. However, the one who holds him back will do so until he is taken out of the way. (2 Thess. 2:6–7)

Paul reminds the Thessalonians that they know about the restraining ministry against the Antichrist's revelation: "And so you know what holds him back." I will outline the direction of Paul's argument on this topic.

The Thessalonians were under the false impression that the day of the Lord was occurring at the time of Paul's writing. To correct their error, Paul instructs that, before the Lord's revelation happens, the Antichrist's revelation will occur first. But Paul explains that, even before the Antichrist's revelation, the individual who restrains this revelation must be first taken away. Paul describes the Antichrist's revelation as being restrained at this time, implying that God's sovereign purpose will unfold at the appointed time: "so that [the Antichrist] will be revealed in his own time." Then Paul explains that the principle of the hidden power of lawlessness is already in the world even though the man of lawlessness has not been revealed. "For the hidden power of lawlessness is already at work." Some translations render "hidden power" as "mystery." This hidden power of lawlessness will one day go unhindered. "[T]he one who holds him back will do so until he is taken out of the way." This tells us there is a figure who is restraining the embodiment of lawlessness, but in due time his restraining ministry will cease. The concealed power of lawlessness will then become the disclosed power of lawlessness embodied in the man of lawlessness, the Antichrist. Traditionally, the enigmatic figure who restrains has been properly designated "the restrainer." Once the restrainer is removed, this causes the Antichrist to be revealed, eventuating in the Antichrist taking his seat in the temple and proclaiming himself as God (2 Thess. 2:4). When this happens at the midpoint, the unabated great tribulation will commence (cf. Rev. 12:12, 17).[7]

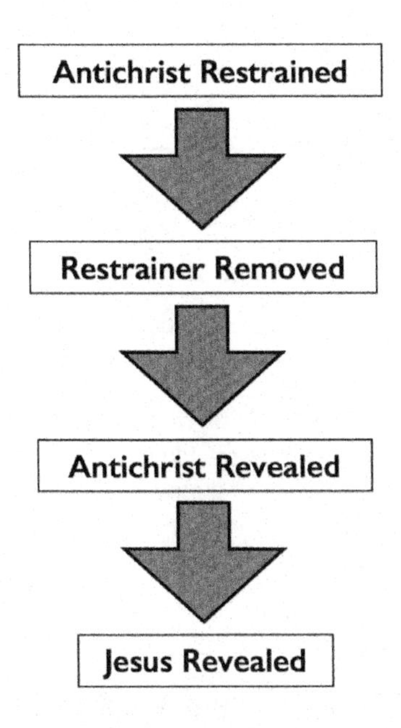

The Antichrist's Ultimate Destruction

> [When the restrainer is removed] then that lawless one will be revealed whom the Lord will slay with the breath of His mouth and bring to an end by the appearance of His coming. (2 Thess. 2:8 NASB)

Paul only mentions the Antichrist coming to his end when the Lord returns. It was not Paul's purpose to describe the complex series of parousia judgments that debilitate the Antichrist's power and lead to his final demise; for this we have to look elsewhere. The book of Revelation, as we will later see, shows that the trumpet and bowl judgments diminish the Antichrist's power, with the battle of Armageddon bringing about his ultimate demise (see Rev. 19:19–20).

ANTICHRIST'S PHASED-OUT REIGN

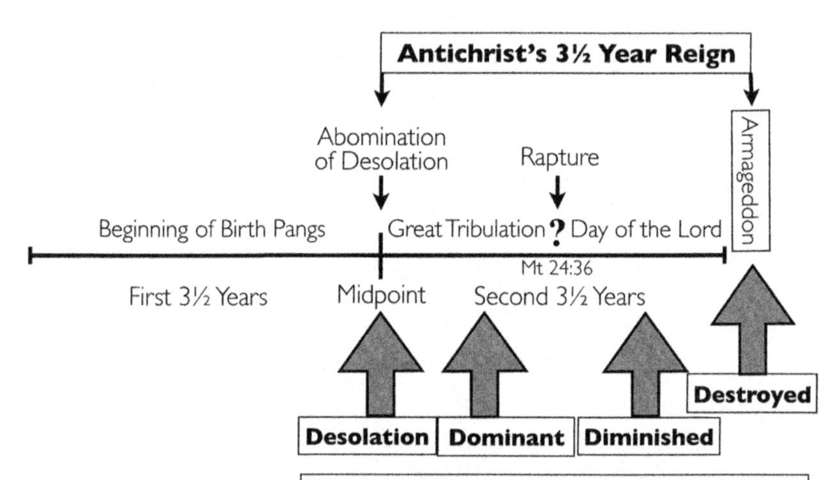

Satanic Possession and Deceptive Miracles

I would be remiss if I gave the Antichrist too much credit for his opposition against God. The real enemy is Satan, who has been opposed to God ever since the garden of Eden. In the garden, Satan deceived our first parents, but he will deceive the entire world in his eschatological possession of the man of lawlessness.

> The arrival of the lawless one will be by Satan's working with all kinds of miracles and signs and false wonders, and with every kind of evil deception directed against those who are perishing, because they found no place in their hearts for the truth so as to be saved. (2 Thess. 2:9–10; cf. Rev. 12:12, 17)

Paul gives a parenthetical description of Satan's intentions and his means of attempting to achieve his diabolical goal. The revelation of the Antichrist will be a key event for Satan's purposes.

Certainly the world is not going to worship an individual simply because he claims to be God. False believers will not apostatize without a powerful deception and real threat. There must be something that convinces the world—albeit deceptively—to give him their allegiance.

Out of the twenty-four instances of the term *parousia* in the New Testament, 2 Thessalonians 2:9 is the only one that refers to the Antichrist's parousia, rendered here as "arrival." It will not be that the Antichrist's coming is merely influenced by Satan; rather, the expression "by Satan's working [*energeia*]" conveys Satanic *possession.* Satan will use deceptive "miracles and signs and false wonders" (cf. Mark 13:22). This will help the Antichrist position himself with power and credibility when he takes his seat in the temple proclaiming himself to be God. George Eldon Ladd captures this well when he says,

> The manifestations of evil which have marked human history will at the end of the age be concentrated in one final incarnation of evil, a "super-man," the Antichrist, who will exercise a world-wide rule, deify the state and achieve a union of church and state so that men will be forced to worship him or suffer economic sanctions and death. Antichrist, energized by satanic powers, will especially direct his hostility against God and the people of God. During his ascendency, there will befall God's people the most fearful persecution history has witnessed.[8]

In conclusion, Paul has given us one of the clearest passages in all of Scripture instructing that the church will be here during the period of the Antichrist. The Thessalonians needed to be taught that the Lord's return had not yet occurred—the Antichrist and the apostasy must come first. Pretribulationism, which claims that the rapture will occur before the Antichrist, renders Paul's teaching unintelligible, making his warnings to the Thessalonians a mere academic exercise. Not to mention, if the day of the Lord starts at the beginning of the seven-year period as pretribulationists claim, then it makes no sense that Paul would give prominence to the revelation of the Antichrist that happens at the midpoint.

Paul directs his teaching to believers because the deception through the Antichrist will be experienced by the last generation of the church. If the church is to be raptured before the Antichrist, why does Paul so passionately warn believers concerning the Antichrist's deception at his revelation? He could have simply told them that the day of the Lord cannot happen until the rapture occurs first. Instead Paul instructs them that the revelation of the Antichrist and the apostasy are evidence that the day of the Lord—and by extension being "gathered" to Christ at the rapture—has not yet come because he expects the last generation of the church to see it transpire. Since we have not seen the revelation of the Antichrist and the apostasy, the Lord has not returned; therefore, there is no need to be "shaken from your composure or disturbed."

TWO RELATED EVENTS *BEFORE* THE DAY OF THE LORD

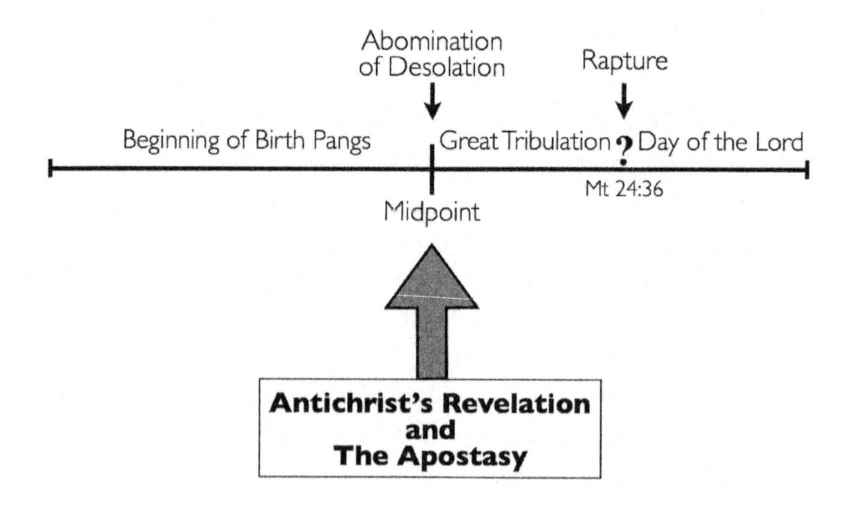

Book of Revelation on the Two Great Acts of Deception

Revelation 13 gives us a fuller composite of Satan's activity behind the great tribulation. This passage teaches that there will be two great acts of deception for the purpose of inducing the world to worship the Antichrist.

First is the counterfeit resurrection of the Antichrist:

> One of the beast's heads appeared to have been killed, but the lethal wound had been healed. And the whole world followed the beast in amazement; they worshiped the dragon because he had given ruling authority to the beast, and they worshiped the beast too, saying: "Who is like the beast?" and "Who is able to make war against him?" (Rev. 13:3–4)

Second is the false prophet performing supernatural signs:

> He exercised all the ruling authority of the first beast on his behalf, and made the earth and those who inhabit it worship the first beast, the one whose lethal wound had been healed. He performed momentous signs, even making fire come down from heaven in front of people and, by the signs he was permitted to perform on behalf of the beast, he deceived those who live on the earth. (Rev. 13:12–14)

These two acts of deception will not be David Copperfield magic. They will be genuine Satan-inspired signs intended to deceive the world into worshiping the Antichrist and thus Satan himself. The instruments that Satan and the Antichrist will impose upon the world to guarantee worship are the twofold image and mark. The most notorious and enigmatic passage in the book of Revelation reads,

> He told those who live on the earth to make an image to the beast who had been wounded by the sword, but still lived. The second beast was empowered to give life to the image of

> the first beast so that it could speak, and could cause all those who did not worship the image of the beast to be killed. He also caused everyone (small and great, rich and poor, free and slave) to obtain a mark on their right hand or on their forehead. Thus no one was allowed to buy or sell things unless he bore the mark of the beast—that is, his name or his number. This calls for wisdom: Let the one who has insight calculate the beast's number, for it is man's number, and his number is 666. (Rev. 13:14–18)

The choice is clear: Partake of the Antichrist's unholy sacrament and live under his short-lived reign or refuse his worship and be killed for Christ's name and live under Christ's reign forever. God will not accept any exceptions for those who capitulate by taking the mark. The following solemn pronouncement should put the fear of God into any Spirit-filled believer:

> A third angel followed the first two, declaring in a loud voice: "If anyone worships the beast and his image, and takes the mark on his forehead or his hand, that person will also drink of the wine of God's anger that has been mixed undiluted in the cup of his wrath, and he will be tortured with fire and sulfur in front of the holy angels and in front of the Lamb. And the smoke from their torture will go up forever and ever, and those who worship the beast and his image will have no rest day or night, along with anyone who receives the mark of his name." This requires the steadfast endurance of the saints—those who obey God's commandments and hold to their faith in Jesus. (Rev. 14:9–12)

Situating the Seven Seals

In the final section of Part 1, I want to conclude by highlighting from the book of Revelation the fourth and fifth seals, which depict martyrs dying during the great tribulation. But first I will preface some comments on the first three seals. (For the structure of the book of Revelation, see the appendix "Proposed Structure to the Book of Revelation.")

The book of Revelation describes a scroll sealed with seven "seals" that are conditions required for the scroll to be opened and the contents of the day of the Lord's wrath to be executed as expressed through the trumpet and bowl judgments. There is a logical progression in the seven seals. As I will argue below, the most plausible scenario is that the first three seals occur during the first half of the seven-year period *before* the great tribulation; the fourth and fifth seals occur *during* the great tribulation; the sixth seal occurs toward the *end* of the great tribulation, signaling the impending day of the Lord; and the seventh seal occurs immediately *after* the great tribulation, pronouncing the day of the Lord's wrath.

We should, however, recognize a spectrum of certainty in this progression. What do I mean by this? Concerning the first three seals, I think we are least certain as to when they will occur during (maybe even before) the seven-year period. My purpose in this section is to focus on the fourth and fifth seals, which we are more certain about, as they are happening during the great tribulation. Since the Antichrist's revelation occurs during the great tribulation, which is a focal event in this book, I will keep my comments on the first three seals to a minimum. In Parts 2 and 3, I will address the last two seals, the sixth and the seventh, about which we possess the greatest degree of certainty since they close out the great tribulation and introduce the day of the Lord's wrath, respectively.

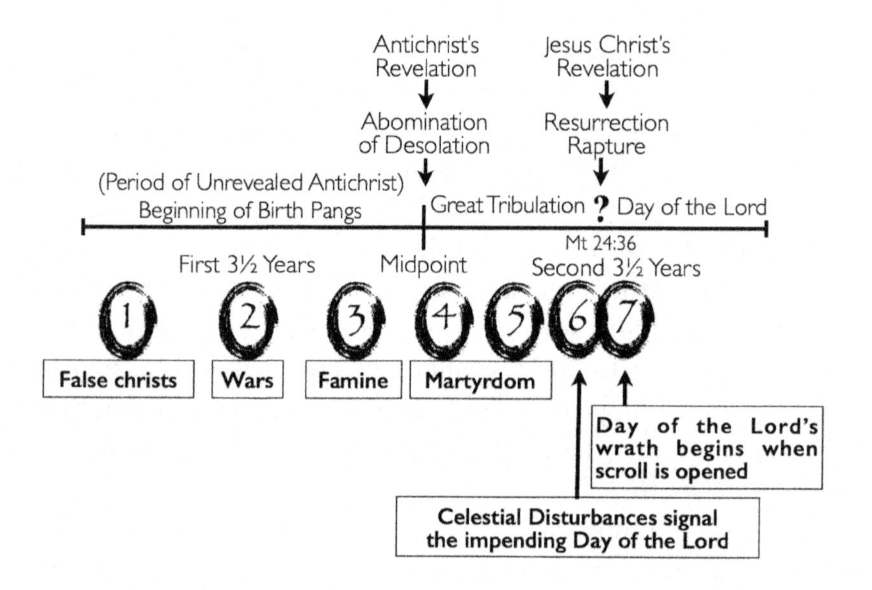

John records the portrayal of the first three seals:

> I looked on when the Lamb opened one of the seven seals, and I heard one of the four living creatures saying with a thunderous voice, "Come!" So I looked, and here came a white horse! The one who rode it had a bow, and he was given a crown, and as a conqueror he rode out to conquer. Then when the Lamb opened the second seal, I heard the second living creature saying, "Come!" And another horse, fiery red, came out, and the one who rode it was granted permission to take peace from the earth, so that people would butcher one another, and he was given a huge sword. Then when the Lamb opened the third seal I heard the third living creature saying, "Come!" So I looked, and here came a black horse! The one who rode it had a balance scale in his hand. Then I heard something like a voice from among the four living creatures saying, "A quart of wheat will cost a day's pay and three quarts of barley will cost a day's pay. But do not damage the olive oil and the wine!" (Rev. 6:1–6)

Incidentally, it should be noted that these first three seals parallel the beginning of birth pangs in Jesus' Olivet Discourse (see Matt. 24:4–8). But the parallels will not stop there. In our study, we will further learn that the other seals correspond to the sequence in Jesus' teaching.

The first seal is the most ambiguous of the seven. Certainly there is an emerging conquering figure, but who is he? Various proposals have been offered, the two most common candidates being Christ and the Antichrist. I think there are good reasons to see the first seal as representing the Antichrist, who is the archetypal false christ.[9] If it does represent the Antichrist, it would not represent him at the time of his revelation at the midpoint but most likely as he comes on the political scene at the beginning of the seven-year period when he is still unrevealed to the world. If this is correct, then it suggests that the second, third, and fourth seals are *phases* of the Antichrist's campaign, with the fourth seal representing his persecution program during the great tribulation.

The second seal (indicating wars) may symbolize a military phase in the Antichrist's campaign, reflecting the time when he establishes himself as a military world leader, consolidating his power base. The fiery red color of the horse likely represents bloodshed since the second seal indicates international wars (he will "take peace from the earth"). Throughout history there have always been wars here and there, including world wars, but the language associated with the second seal conveys an intensification of war, perhaps a world war on an unprecedented scale.

The third seal results in famine and scarcity, which may be the consequence of battle in the war-torn areas the Antichrist conquers. The black horse of this seal symbolizes famine. The imagery of a balance scale symbolizes high prices and rationing of food due to scarcity (cf. Ezek. 4:16; Lev. 36:26). Another indication of famine is the description of the value of the wheat and barley as eight to sixteen times the average prices in the Roman Empire at the time. In an eschatological context, this will be inflation to an acute degree.[10] This food crisis may allow the

Antichrist to assert his control over food prices and related commodities. How would he eventually do this? Presumably, the crisis would carry over into the second half of the seven-year period, and when the Antichrist institutes his mark-of-the-beast scheme, he will use it to assume absolute control of who can buy and sell.

The Fourth Seal—Means of Killing

> Then when the Lamb opened the fourth seal I heard the voice of the fourth living creature saying, "Come!" So I looked and here came a pale green horse! The name of the one who rode it was Death, and Hades followed right behind. They were given authority over a fourth of the earth, to kill its population with the sword, famine, and disease, and by the wild animals of the earth. (Rev. 6:7–8)

The fourth and most certainly the fifth seal represent martyrdom during the great tribulation. It is my contention that the fourth seal reflects the consequences of refusing to take the Antichrist's mark. This will be a dark time for believers. They will need to trust God completely for physical and spiritual sustenance (Matt. 6:25–34). The fourth seal shifts perspective from the world at large to a more limited scope. This final horse is pale green, symbolizing death, personified by the final rider with Hades following him. Authority was given to these two personified, malevolent forces by God's permission to kill by various means—sword, famine, pestilence, and wild beasts of the earth.[11] This authority is limited to "over a fourth of the earth." To be sure, the expression "to kill" suggests intention. It doesn't mean that this intention is accomplished. In contrast, the book of Revelation will actually state when such a massive number of people are killed; for example, "A third of humanity was killed by these three plagues, that is, by the fire, the smoke, and the sulfur that came out of their mouths" (Rev. 9:18; cf. 11:13). The question is whether one-fourth of the earth is geographic or demographic.

The fourth seal is not clear on this point. However, the fifth seal is likely a result of the fourth seal; but we should not assume that one-fourth of the earth are martyrs. It may refer just to Christendom in general. Nevertheless, the Antichrist will likely control the entire globe politically and religiously (Rev. 13:3, 7–8; Dan. 7:23); but in God's sovereignty, his intent to kill may be restricted. In this context, the fourth seal would be the means of killing and the fifth seal would be the result.

Next, the passage says that Death and Hades will use "wild beasts of the earth" to kill. It is significant that the term for "beasts" (*thērion*) is used thirty-nine times in the book of Revelation. In every instance, it refers to the Antichrist or his associations (his image, system, or religious accomplice). This is the first time the term is used. Since it refers to the Antichrist and his associations in the remaining thirty-eight instances, it would be very unusual, though not impossible, for it not to refer to the Antichrist and his religious associations here, as well. In addition, there is a definite article "the" (*ho*) that precedes "beasts," which makes the beasts *definite*. In other words, it is not referring to beasts as a general class; instead, the presence of the article indicates particularity.[12] Later we learn that the book of Revelation explicitly states that the beast is, in fact, responsible for putting believers to death. "If anyone is meant for captivity, into captivity he will go. If anyone is to be killed by the sword, then by the sword he must be killed. This requires steadfast endurance and faith from the saints" (Rev. 13:10; cf. Rev. 20:4).

It is not surprising that Hades is said to follow close behind Death. A combination of Old Testament usage of these terms reveals that they are basically synonymous (e.g. Ps. 6:5; 49:14; 116:3; Prov. 2:18; 5:5; 7:27; Job 33:22; 38:17). Another connection between the paired Antichrist and false prophet with Death and Hades is that both pairs are thrown into the lake of fire (Rev. 19:20; 20:10, 14).

In summary, I suggest that the fourth seal represents a choice people must make. In the book of Revelation, the overarching choice for everyone on earth is to follow the Antichrist or Jesus

Christ (cf. Rev. 13; 14:9–13). Those who follow Christ risk death by "sword, famine-pestilence, and by wild beasts," the consequences for not following the Antichrist.

The Fifth Seal—Result of Killing and Promise of God's Wrath

> Now when the Lamb opened the fifth seal, I saw under the altar the souls of those who had been violently killed because of the word of God and because of the testimony they had given. They cried out with a loud voice, "How long, Sovereign Master, holy and true, before you judge those who live on the earth and avenge our blood?" Each of them was given a long white robe and they were told to rest for a little longer, until the full number was reached of both their fellow servants and their brothers who were going to be killed just as they had been. (Rev. 6:9–11)

The fifth seal depicts the result *and* the ongoing killings of the Antichrist. The martyrs are portrayed as crying out for justice concerning their wrongful deaths, asking their sovereign God when his wrath will be poured out to vindicate them. John sees "under the altar the souls of those who had been violently killed because of the word of God and because of the testimony they had given" (Rev. 6:9).

The fifth seal is problematic for the pretribulational interpretation, which sees all the seals as expressions of the day of the Lord's wrath, because the fifth seal explicitly applies to believers, not unbelievers. To be more specific, it applies to *martyred* believers! The pretribulational interpretation by necessity has believers suffering the wrath of God. This contradicts the biblical promise that believers will not experience God's wrath. "For God did not destine us for wrath but for gaining salvation through our Lord Jesus Christ" (1 Thess. 5:9).

In addition, the fifth seal clearly states that, even at the time of their martyrdom, the wrath of God has not arrived yet.

> They cried out with a loud voice, "How long, Sovereign Master, holy and true, *before you judge* those who live on the earth and avenge our blood?" Each of them was given a long white robe and they were told to *rest for a little longer, until* the full number was reached of both their fellow servants and their brothers who were going to be killed just as they had been. (Rev. 6:10–11, emphasis mine)

The fifth seal martyrs recognize that they did not die as a result of God's wrath; instead they are crying out to God asking when he will avenge their blood. This is confirmed with a heavenly promise that God's wrath will occur very soon; but before this onset, the providential fulfillment of martyrdom must be reached. In the meantime, martyred souls are given long white robes and told "to rest for a little longer." Long white robes are a guarantee of the resurrection hope soon to take place. In Part 2, we will see that after the sixth seal is opened this resurrection promise is fulfilled: "an enormous crowd that no one could count, made up of persons from every nation, tribe, people, and language, standing before the throne and before the Lamb dressed in long white robes" (Rev. 7:9, cf. vv. 13–14). The fifth seal is pivotal because, while it is the goal of the Antichrist to kill Christians, the giving of white robes to martyrs points to God's impending vindication (cf. Rom. 12:19; cf. Luke 18:7–8).

The Antichrist's Woes, then God's Wrath	
Seals 1–4	The Woes: False Christs, War, Famine, Martyrdom
Seal 5	Effect of the Woes: Death
Seal 6	God's Wrath Signaled: Celestial Disturbances
Seal 7	God's Wrath Expressed: Trumpets and Bowls

Conclusion

In Part 1, I started by explaining some preliminaries about the Antichrist and situating his actions in a seven-year period. The Antichrist's revelation will occur at the midpoint, followed by his great tribulation against the church. The warning to the church is not to apostatize; instead we are called to persevere in faith during the unequaled persecution and acute deception. After I expounded on Jesus' and Paul's instructions on the great tribulation, I concluded with an explanation of the first five seals in the book of Revelation, focusing on the fourth and fifth seals.

In Part 2, "The Rapture of God's People," I will show that a unique cluster of celestial events will signal to the world God's impending wrath, as well as signal to the church her impending deliverance. During this celestial upheaval and blackout, the great tribulation will be cut short with the Lord's brilliant return in the clouds to resurrect his people and deliver those who have remained alive up to his return, rapturing both groups to meet him in the air.

PART 2.
The Rapture of God's People

At some point toward the end of the great tribulation a cluster of unique celestial disturbances will cause an upheaval and global blackout. Then the Lord will radiantly return in the clouds to resurrect his people and deliver believers who remain alive, rapturing both groups to meet him in the air. In Part 2, I will first consider this unique cluster of celestial disturbances that will signal to the church her impending deliverance from the great tribulation and signal to the world God's impending wrath. Then I will focus on the rapture event described by Jesus, Paul, and the book of Revelation. Each contributes an important element to the larger picture of God's eschatological deliverance.

The Great Tribulation 'Cut Short'

In God's providential timing, he will "cut short" the great tribulation for the sake of the elect. This cutting short, we will see, is by means of the rapture. Jesus prophesies,

> "For then there will be great suffering unlike anything that has happened from the beginning of the world until now, or ever

> will happen. And if those days had not been cut short, no one would be saved [i.e. delivered]. But for the sake of the elect those days will be cut short." (Matt. 24:21–22)

The expression "those days" is not denoting literal days, as if each twenty-four-hour day is itself shortened, for example, to a twenty-hour day. Nor does it mean that the seven-year period is shortened. Rather, the phrase "those days" refers to the time of persecution. The great tribulation against believers will be cut short, otherwise "no one would be saved [i.e. delivered]." This cutting short is by means of physical deliverance, not spiritual salvation; to be sure, our glorified bodies are a vital part of our spiritual salvation. The New American Standard Bible has a better rendering: "no life would have been saved." If the persecution were allowed to reach the Antichrist's intended goal, every believer would be exterminated. Jesus reveals the purpose for the shortening: "for the sake of the elect" (cf. v. 31). The Greek term for "cut short" is *koloboō,* which means "to reduce the duration of something, shorten," and can generally connote amputating or preventing something from reaching its full-intended length. When the Antichrist's great tribulation is cut short, it will allow sufficient time for God to unleash his day-of-the-Lord wrath throughout the remainder of the seven-year period, which includes, for example, the fifth trumpet judgment that lasts five months (Rev. 9:5).

In relation to the second half of the seven-year period, exactly when will this cutting short (resulting from the coming of Christ) occur? We cannot know because Jesus says, "But as for that day and hour no one knows it—not even the angels in heaven—except the Father alone" (Matt. 24:36). What we can know, however, is that the great tribulation begins at the midpoint of the seven years when the Antichrist causes an abomination of desolation, setting himself up in a temple-like structure and commanding the world to worship him (cf. Dan. 9:27; 2 Thess. 2:3–4). Accordingly, the most we can know is that the cutting short will happen *sometime during the second half of the seven-year period.* But we will not know the day nor the hour.[13]

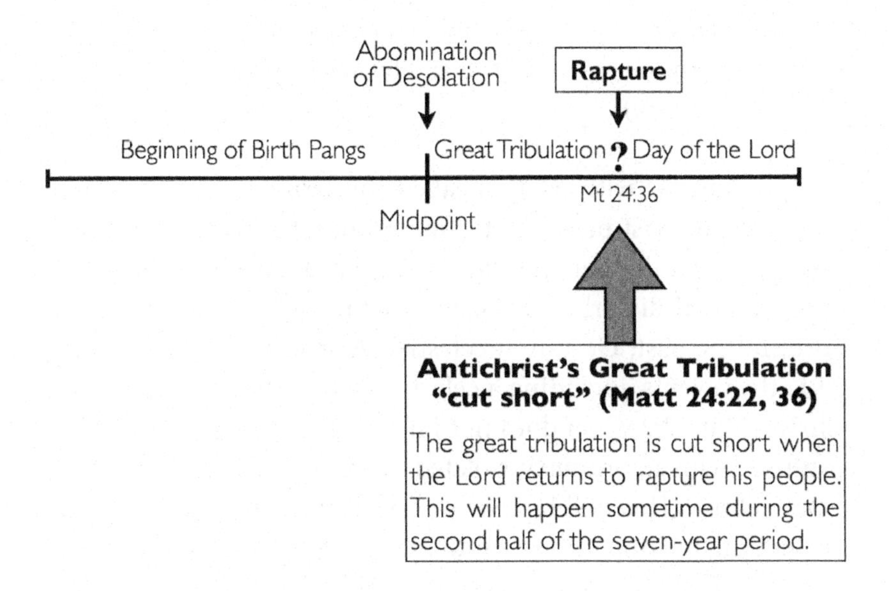

The Celestial Disturbance Event

The celestial disturbance is a frequent theme in the Bible, so it is incumbent upon us to pay attention to what it is trying to tell us. Christ is not just going to arrive on the clouds without any warning to the world. He will use a harbinger to announce his impending judgment and deliverance. This celestial event will be anything but inconspicuous, for the Lord will use the heavenly bodies to cause a celestial salvo.

> "Immediately after the suffering of those days, the sun will be darkened, and the moon will not give its light; the stars will fall from heaven, and the powers of heaven will be shaken." (Matt. 24:29)

Most certainly Jesus has in mind Joel's prophecy of an explicit sign to the eschatological day of the Lord.

> I will produce portents both in the sky and on the earth—blood, fire, and columns of smoke. The sunlight will be turned to darkness and the moon to the color of blood, before the day of the Lord comes—that great and terrible day! (Joel 2:30–31; cf. Isa. 13:9–10)

Joel provides us with what is called the *terminus a quo*, which means the earliest possible starting point for something. In our case, Joel reveals that the day of the Lord cannot begin until these celestial disturbances happen first—*before* the day of the Lord. In the past, God used celestial signs to mark out seasons and other events, including a celestial sign to the first coming of Christ (Matt. 2:2). Joel does not intend this celestial event to be confused with an ordinary, isolated occurrence such as a solar or lunar eclipse. This will be a *cluster* of disturbed celestial bodies portending the impending wrath of God. It will be unprecedented so the world will not mistake it.

CELESTIAL SIGN ANNOUNCES THE DAY OF THE LORD

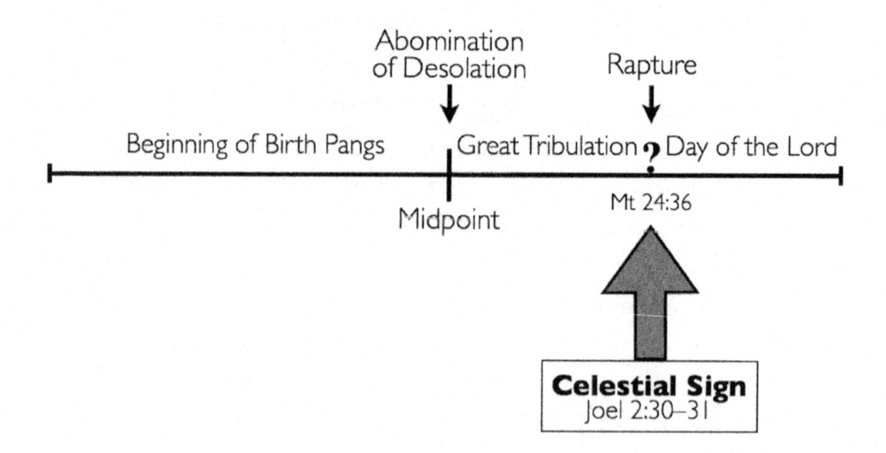

While Joel explicitly specifies that this celestial disturbance will signal the day of the Lord, Jesus adds another piece of information. Matthew 24:29 begins with "*immediately after* the suffering of those days." What days? The days of great tribulation (vv.

21–22). God will cut short the days of great tribulation with the celestial disturbances in conjunction with Jesus' coming.

What will be the exact nature of these celestial events? It is likely that the falling stars refer to meteors and the moon turning blood red and the sun darkening will be caused by an earthly cataclysmic disaster, possibly volcanoes (or worse, a super volcano). In any case, it will not be a single celestial event. It will be multiple events functioning together as a salvo of havoc, signaling the day of the Lord as unmistakable. Luke provides a foreboding picture.

> "And there will be signs in the sun and moon and stars, and on the earth nations will be in distress, anxious over the roaring of the sea and the surging waves. People will be fainting from fear and from the expectation of what is coming on the world, for the powers of the heavens will be shaken. Then they will see the Son of Man arriving in a cloud with power and great glory. But when these things begin to happen, stand up and raise your heads, because your redemption is drawing near." (Luke 21:25–28)

Luke highlights that there will be polar responses to the celestial disturbance event from two types of people. The ungodly will be in "distress, anxious . . . fainting from fear and from the expectation of what is coming on the world." The godly, however, are exhorted to "stand up and raise your heads, because your redemption is drawing near."

Luke also develops the celestial composite picture by adding an earthly element. He records Jesus as saying, "and on the earth nations will be in distress, anxious over the roaring of the sea and the surging waves." Nations do not distress over mere ten-foot waves, so this suggests a global impact. Waves of terrifying size may be caused by meteors crashing into the seas, or this may be tsunami language. Interestingly, the Greek term for "surging waves" (*salos*) can mean "earthquake." For a tsunami to cause distress on a global scale, it would have to be caused by a gigantic earthquake or a cluster of regional earthquakes. So, more descriptively, we could call the sign to the day of the Lord's wrath the "earthly-celestial" disturbances.

The Sixth Seal Signals Impending Wrath

This leads us to our final (and most descriptive) celestial passage of the sixth seal, which is found in the book of Revelation.

> Then I looked when the Lamb opened the sixth seal, and a huge earthquake took place; the sun became as black as sackcloth made of hair, and the full moon became blood red; and the stars in the sky fell to the earth like a fig tree dropping its unripe figs when shaken by a fierce wind. The sky was split apart like a scroll being rolled up, and every mountain and island was moved from its place. Then the kings of the earth, the very important people, the generals, the rich, the powerful, and everyone, slave and free, hid themselves in the caves and among the rocks of the mountains. They said to the mountains and to the rocks, "Fall on us and hide us from the face of the one who is seated on the throne and from the wrath of the Lamb, because the great day of their wrath has come, and who is able to withstand it?" (Rev. 6:12–17; cf. Isa. 24:18–20)

When the sixth seal is opened, an immense earthquake will take place, adding an earthly element to these unmistakable and global visible signs. This earthquake will likely be universally felt, portending Yahweh's coming to judge the earth. Perhaps it is the cause of what appear to be global tsunamis in Luke's account (Luke 21:25–27).

John uses ominous imagery to describe the sixth seal. "The sun became as black as sackcloth made of hair, and the full moon became blood red." Sackcloth was a coarse material made of black goat's hair, symbolizing soberness and mourning. What will the ungodly be mourning for? Their very lives! The moon will turn an ominously blood-red color. Most likely, the same event causing the sun to darken will also cause the darkening of the moon. The celestial lights will go dark, preparing for the luminous divine-glory to radiate the globe.

Another heavenly element that our Revelation passage portends is the falling of celestial bodies. "The stars in the sky fell to the earth like a fig tree dropping its unripe figs when shaken by a fierce wind." This language may indicate an unprecedented meteor shower. It will be accompanied by the sky being "split apart like a scroll being rolled up, and every mountain and island was moved from its place." This language can also describe the sky that "could no longer be seen [*apochōrizō*]."[14] This exceptional imagery of the sky splitting apart or disappearing probably serves the purpose of disclosing to the ungodly the presence of God in heaven, for in the very next sentence the ungodly cry, "Hide us from the face of the one who is seated on the throne and from the wrath of the Lamb." The term for "face" is *prosōpon*, which can mean a literal face or someone's personal presence. This "presence," combined with the upheaval all around them, will cause them to try to flee from God. So, during the sixth seal, God will split the sky to disclose his presence from heaven to be seen by the ungodly. This event is classically apocalyptic. The sky splitting apart, certainly, would be one of the most jaw-dropping elements in this celestial overture. This will pave the way for Jesus' descent from heaven to gather his people to himself (Matt. 24:30; cf. 1 Thess. 4:16–17; Acts 1:11; Rev. 1:7).

In response to the sixth-seal upheaval, John narrates the reaction of the ungodly:

> Then the kings of the earth, the very important people, the generals, the rich, the powerful, and everyone, slave and free, hid themselves in the caves and among the rocks of the mountains. They said to the mountains and to the rocks, "Fall on us and hide us from the face of the one who is seated on the throne and from the wrath of the Lamb, because the great day of their wrath has come, and who is able to withstand it?" (Rev. 6:15–17; cf. Isa. 2:10–11, 19–21)

This reaction recalls Luke's account of how they will respond: "fainting from fear and from the expectation of what is coming on the world, for the powers of the heavens will be shaken" (Luke 21:26). This upheaval will affect the gamut of social classes, showing no preferential treatment for anyone. Social status will not save anyone from God's wrath at the end of their lives. The ungodly will not interpret the sixth seal as naturally freakish. They will see it as portending *divine retribution*. In verses 15–17, the ungodly try to hide—even asking to be killed—so as to escape the impending wrath (*orgē*) of God.

If God calls you to live in the last generation of the church to encounter the Antichrist's great tribulation, what will your reaction be to this cataclysmic celestial disturbance that shakes the heavens? Will you "faint from terror, apprehensive of what is coming on the world"? Or, as I hope, will you be faithful and confident to "stand up and lift up your heads, because your redemption is drawing near"?

By comparing Scripture with Scripture, we have been able to establish a composite picture of this celestial event. The consistency among Joel, Jesus, and the book of Revelation demonstrates that this event signals the looming day of the Lord. It will engender two opposite reactions: terror for the wicked and triumph for the godly. Only when this celestial condition occurs will the rapture event actually be imminent. Not before then! The rapture of God's people is the event we will take up next.

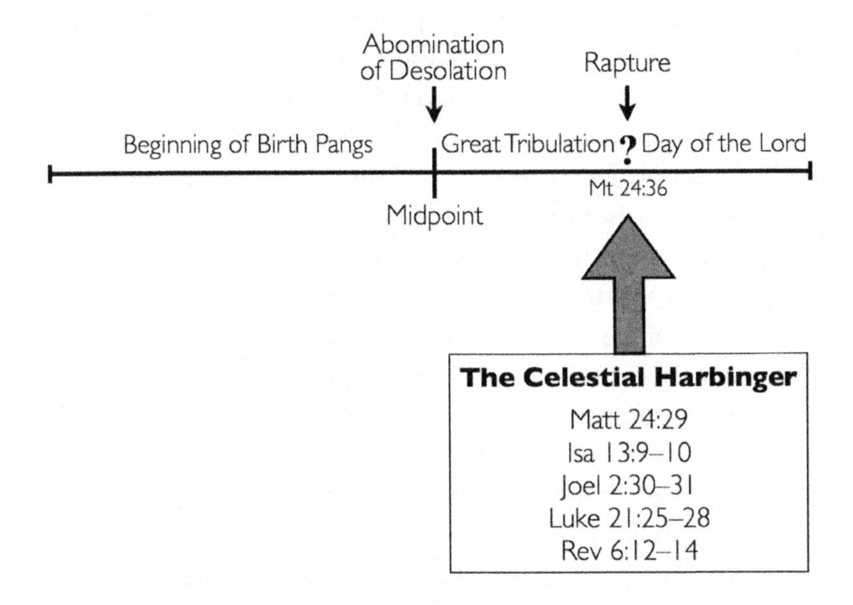

Shekinah Sign and Jesus Arriving on the Clouds

Up to Matthew 24:27, Jesus has not answered the disciples' question about the sign of his coming and the end of the age (cf. Matt. 24:3). Jesus prophesied about the preliminary birth pangs that will affect the world at large, and he warned his disciples that great suffering for God's people would precede his return. Now, in verse 27, he finally reveals the specific sign of his coming: "For just like the lightning comes from the east and flashes to the west, so the coming of the Son of Man will be." This verse begins with "for" (*gar*), which gives the reason the disciples are not to believe people when they say, "Here is the Christ!" or "There he is!" (cf. Matt. 24:23–26). The lightning imagery denotes his Shekinah glory, the radiant glory of his divine presence (cf. "His lightning bolts light up the world; the earth sees and trembles," Ps. 97:4). When it happens, there will be no need to point it out because it will be unmistakable. The directional analogy of flashing from the east to the west indicates the universal visibility of the event.

The Shekinah glory will be the authenticating sign of the genuine Messiah, contrasting it with false messianic claimants.

In conjunction with Jesus explaining the sign, he ominously utters the proverb, "Wherever the corpse is, there the vultures will gather" (Matt. 24:28). This verse is related to what came before it and what comes after it. It is a pivotal structural verse in that it distinguishes two epochs of human history, conveying the principle that where moral corruption exists, divine judgment is required. When the world's depravity has reached full to the brim, God's eschatological judgment will begin. This comports with the narrative structure of Matthew 24 because everything preceding verse 28 describes moral corruption, and everything following it describes divine judgment. In short, the proverb serves as a warning that the day of the Lord's judgment will begin when Christ returns. There may be an additional point to this proverb, as well. People will no more miss the presence of the Son of Man when he returns than vultures will miss the presence of corpses. Jesus' return will be obvious.

At some point during the celestial spine-chilling darkness, global-seismic quakes, and tempestuous seas, the Lord will pierce through in all of his theophanic, Shekinah splendor.

> "Then the sign of the Son of Man will appear in heaven, and all the tribes of the earth will mourn. They will see the Son of Man arriving on the clouds of heaven with power and great glory." (Matt. 24:30)

This parousia-glory authenticates Christ's presence, contrary to the false signs originating from inauthentic christs. To accentuate the brilliant sign, the Shekinah glory is revealed against the backdrop of the dark celestial disturbances. (Other related verses that mention Christ's appearance are 1 Timothy 6:14; 2 Timothy 4:8; Titus 2:13; Acts 2:20; 1 John 2:28; 1 John 3:2; Colossians 3:4; 1 Peter 5:4; and Revelation 1:7.) The Greek term for "heaven" (*ouranos*) in this context refers to the sky rather than the abode of God because it depicts Jesus' descent with clouds. That the nations ("tribes") of the earth will see him indicates that this is not a localized event but a global appearance (cf. Rev. 1:7). The nations will not repent. They will mourn, knowing that Jesus is coming as judge. The clouds are vehicles of transportation. In antiquity they were a cachet of deity—Jesus is the divine cloud-rider. His appearance at his return will be the *par excellence* of theophanies, for it will be the global and definitive revelation bringing this present age to completion.

THE SIGN TO THE PAROUSIA

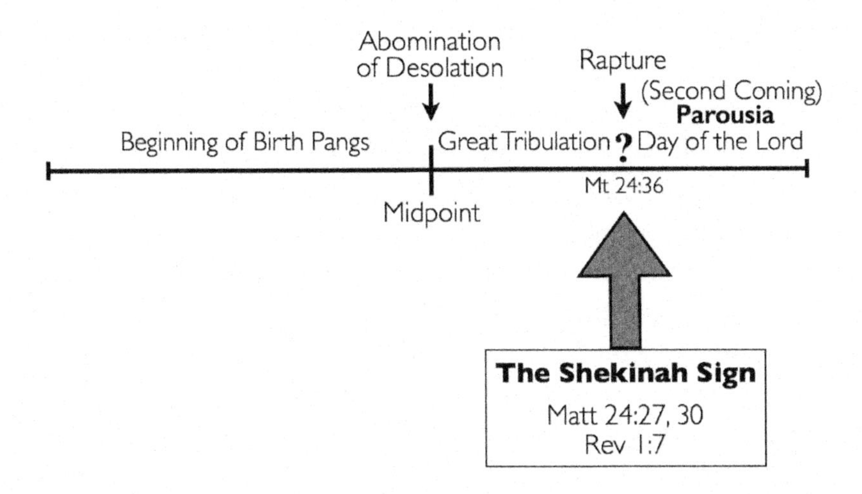

'Gather His Elect'

The celestial disturbance event will signal to the entire world the impending day of the Lord. This will be followed by the glorious-manifestation sign of Christ's coming when he descends through the sky. At this point, the great tribulation is cut short when Jesus' angels "gather his elect."

> "And he will send his angels with a loud trumpet blast, and they will gather his elect from the four winds, from one end of heaven to the other." (Matt. 24:31)

At Christ's ascension, he scattered his elect witnesses to the corners of the earth. "But you will receive power when the Holy Spirit has come upon you, and you will be my witnesses in Jerusalem, and in all Judea and Samaria, and to the farthest parts of the earth" (Acts 1:8). At his second coming, Jesus will gather the fruit of his disciples' labor, God's people, from the four winds of the heavens to his presence.

Prewrath contends that the "gather his elect" event in verse 31 is a reference to the rapture, which happens soon after the resurrection. Not everyone agrees, however, including pretribulational and preterist interpreters. Pretribulational theology places the rapture before the great tribulation. They interpret this gathering as the physical gathering of Jews back to the land of Israel when Jesus returns. To be sure, prewrath affirms that there will be a gathering of Jews back to the land of Israel, but it will not happen at this point. Preterist theology interprets this gathering as an event already begun or completed near the year A.D. 70. In contrast to pretribulationism and preterism, prewrath believes that the weight of evidence supports this gathering to be the rapture.

The expression "gather his elect" is an implicit expression, lacking specificity. It was not Jesus' purpose in his Olivet Discourse to expand on this event. The disciples were asking for the identification of the *sign* itself, not what would happen after the sign. I will later consider four reasons why verse 31 is a reference to the rapture. But first we need to walk through the most explicit rapture passage in the Bible given by the apostle Paul in his first epistle to the Thessalonians. This will inform our understanding of the gathering event in Matthew 24:31. This approach makes sense because Paul draws from Jesus' Olivet Discourse for his own teaching on the second coming in his Thessalonian epistles (see the appendix "Parallels between Jesus and Paul").

Situating the Thessalonian Letters

> Now we do not want you to be uninformed, brothers and sisters, about those who are asleep, so that you will not grieve like

> the rest who have no hope. For if we believe that Jesus died and rose again, so also we believe that God will bring with him those who have fallen asleep as Christians. For we tell you this by the word of the Lord, that we who are alive, who are left until the coming of the Lord, will surely not go ahead of those who have fallen asleep. For the Lord himself will come down from heaven with a shout of command, with the voice of the archangel, and with the trumpet of God, and the dead in Christ will rise first. Then we who are alive, who are left, will be suddenly caught up together with them in the clouds to meet the Lord in the air. And so we will always be with the Lord. Therefore encourage one another with these words. (1 Thess. 4:13–18)

The apostle Paul's letters are replete with teachings on the Lord's coming. Most often they are brief passages scattered throughout his thirteen letters with an occasional larger section. Yet he wrote two letters with the exclusive purpose of answering eschatological concerns: the Thessalonian letters. Thessalonica was located in ancient Macedonia, which is present-day Thessaloniki, Greece. Paul visited this city on his second missionary journey and there planted a church that was mostly Gentile. Both of his epistles to this church may have been his first, written about A.D. 50–51. I want to consider Paul's teaching on the classic rapture passage in 1 Thessalonians 4:13–18. Even though this is a popular rapture passage, we should keep in mind the historical concern Paul is addressing: the Thessalonians are grieving hopelessly like the pagans.

Correct Eschatology Matters

Sometime after Paul left Thessalonica, he received a report from Timothy on the situation of the church (1 Thess. 3:6). Presumably, this report contained information that some members had died, causing angst within the church about their destiny since they would not be alive at the Lord's coming. Paul writes back to reassure these new believers that they will be reunited with their deceased loved ones at the parousia. He begins his reassurance, writing,

> Now we do not want you to be uninformed, brothers and sisters, about those who are asleep, so that you will not grieve like the rest who have no hope. (1 Thess. 4:13)

This verse is the most important verse in the epistle because it informs us that Paul's purpose for writing to the grieving Thessalonians was to respond to their ignorance of the relationship between the resurrection and the parousia of Christ. If Paul can accomplish the goal of correcting this ignorance, he believes that the Thessalonians should be comforted in their distress because their manner of grieving is inconsistent with Christian hope.

The ignorance of the Thessalonians prompts Paul to stress that their deceased are not at a disadvantage. It will not only be the survivors at the coming who will be delivered, but the dead in Christ as well. Their loved ones will not only participate in the return of Christ, but they will have the privilege of coming with Christ (as disembodied souls); thereby, the dead in Christ will have the blessing of participating in God's first divine purpose at Christ's parousia, the resurrection. At that time, there will be a reunion of the dead in Christ and the alive in Christ who have survived. Therefore they need to stop grieving like their pagan neighbors who do not possess this certain hope. Paul writes,

> For if we believe that Jesus died and rose again, so also we believe that God will bring with him those who have fallen asleep as Christians. (1 Thess. 4:14)

This verse contains an awkward "if-then" statement. Paul is not saying that *if* we do not believe Jesus died and rose again, *then* God will not cause souls to be brought back with Jesus. Instead, the sense of the condition is since we believe in the truth of the resurrection of Jesus, it *follows theologically* that we should also believe in the resurrection of believers. He teaches the Corinthian believers this same truth: "Now God indeed raised the Lord and he will raise us by his power" (1 Cor. 6:14; cf. 2 Cor. 4:14). At the return of Jesus, the Father will cause all the believing deceased, who exist as disembodied souls, to accompany Jesus from heaven. The destination from heaven to the sky will be made explicit in verses 16–17. The last statement in verse 14, "God will bring with him those who have fallen asleep as Christians," is developed in the next few verses.

Paul on the Resurrection and Rapture

> For we tell you this by the word of the Lord, that we who are alive, who are left until the coming of the Lord, will surely not go ahead of those who have fallen asleep. For the Lord himself will come down from heaven with a shout of command, with the voice of the archangel, and with the trumpet of God, and the dead in Christ will rise first. Then we who are alive, who are left, will be suddenly caught up together with them in the clouds to meet the Lord in the air. And so we will always be with the Lord. Therefore encourage one another with these words. (1 Thess. 4:15–18)

In verse 15, Paul begins to elaborate on God's initial purpose for the return of Jesus, the relationship between the soon-to-be-resurrected and the believers who are alive. Paul notes the source for his authoritative teaching: "by the word of the Lord." This "word" refers to the content in verses 16–18 (verse 15 is Paul's own anticipatory summary). In the Old Testament, the expression "word of the Lord" would have announced a prophetic oracle, but in the New Testament, this expression denotes the gospel itself or a teaching of Jesus during his ministry. In our passage, it is most certain that Paul is drawing from Jesus' Olivet Discourse because of the many parallels he uses.

The second part of verse 15 uses the phrase: "we who are alive, who are left until the coming of the Lord." Paul does not simply say "we who are *alive*," but rather clarifies it with "who are *left* until the coming of the Lord." He uses both of these phrases together again in verse 17. The Greek phrase is *hoi perileipomenoi* ("who are left"). When applied to humans, as it is here, it indicates survival. In addition, this term in biblical, Jewish, and secular usage can mean not just survival, but survival from some tragedy in which others have died.[15] Paul is likely using this term to allude to Jesus' teaching on the great tribulation. Incidentally, the term "asleep" in antiquity was used often as a euphemism for death, but Paul probably gives it a connotation for the future resurrection of believers.

In addition, Paul teaches that those who survive ("who are left *until* the coming of the Lord") live right up to the parousia. This shows there is no gap of time between the rapture and his coming; the rapture is an initial event of the parousia of Christ. Thus Paul envisions the last generation of the church surviving under very difficult circumstances right up to the parousia (cf. 2 Thess. 1:6–7). This is consistent with my earlier discussion on how Jesus describes a surviving remnant experiencing persecution right up to the time of his coming—persecution that will eventually be cut short by that coming (Matt. 24:15; 21–22; 29–31).[16]

The last part of 1 Thessalonians 4:15 states that the living remnant of believers "will surely not go ahead of those who have fallen asleep." This implies that the Thessalonian defective (i.e. uniformed) eschatology was the belief that those alive would be at an advantage at Christ's parousia. Paul, however, stresses that not only will the alive *not* go ahead of the dead in Christ, but the dead in Christ will receive glorified bodies *before* those alive in Christ receive theirs. Accordingly, Paul gives comfort to the Thessalonians by teaching that their dead loved ones in Christ will participate at the parousia, even figuring prominently!

Let us take a step back and see where we are at this point in Paul's reasoning. In verse 13, Paul states the problem: The Thessalonians are grieving hopelessly ("Now we do not want you to be uninformed, brothers and sisters, about those who are asleep, so that you will not grieve like the rest who have no hope"). In verse 14, he provides his main point for comfort ("we believe that God will bring with him those who have fallen asleep as Christians").

In verse 15, he begins to support the main point with a summary of the word of the Lord ("that we who are alive, who are left until the coming of the Lord, will surely not go ahead of those who have fallen asleep"). Now in verses 16–17, Paul gives us the word of the Lord elaborating on the main point:

> For the Lord himself will come down from heaven with a shout of command, with the voice of the archangel, and with the trumpet of God, and the dead in Christ will rise first. Then we who are alive, who are left, will be suddenly caught up together with them in the clouds to meet the Lord in the air. And so we will always be with the Lord. (1 Thess. 4:16–17)

These two verses have given the church the popular rapture teaching, spawning many sermons, songs, and novels. My aim here is to give a careful interpretation of Paul's intention by not allowing the text to say more or less than it does.

First, the passage stresses that it is the Lord *himself* who will descend from heaven to the clouds. The Groom is personally coming for his bride. This is in fulfillment of the angelic prophecy at Christ's ascension in which it was said that he would come back to the sky with theophanic clouds (Acts 1:9–11).

Next, Paul teaches us there will be a triad of glorious, booming sounds accompanying Christ's descent: "with a *shout* of command, with the *voice* of the archangel, and with the *trumpet* of God" (emphasis mine). This will not be a "secret return" of Jesus! Some interpreters have seen this triad as a single sound described three different ways. But most have (rightly) interpreted this in a more natural way as three distinct sounds, with each serving a different function.

The first sound is a shouting command, which suggests that it will come from the Lord himself to "wake" the dead in Christ. During Jesus' earthly ministry he commanded a dead person to come alive in a similar way: "He shouted in a loud voice, 'Lazarus, come out!'" (John 11:43). Jesus' life-creating command foreshadows the macrocosmic resurrection of the saints. In the second sound, Paul notes "the voice of the archangel." We are not given the name of the archangel, and it is difficult to know what role this voice will have. Perhaps the voice will serve to give instructions to the hosts of angels to gather the saints since archangels rule over angels and a host of angels will come with Christ at his return (Matt. 24:31; 2 Thess. 1:7; Luke 9:26). The third sound is "the trumpet of God." Trumpet blasts served different purposes in ancient Israel. They were used for assemblies, warnings, battles, liturgies, and coronation ceremonies (e.g. Num. 10:2–10). An important trumpet of God sounded at Sinai (e.g. Exod. 19:16; 20:18). In our immediate context, the trumpet is related to the resurrection and gathering of all God's people.

We need to be particularly careful here since the Bible mentions different eschatological trumpets that will be blown. We should not be quick to assume that every trumpet blast is the same. The passage says it is the "trumpet of God," which emphasizes the possessive nature, giving it a decreeing action. There are two parallel passages having the same trumpet in view.

> "He will send his angels with a loud trumpet blast, and they will gather his elect from the four winds, from one end of heaven to the other." (Matt. 24:31)

Jesus calls it a "loud trumpet blast." We know that it is the same trumpet call as in 1 Thessalonians 4:16 because Jesus also teaches that it will be blown at his descent when the parousia begins, with both passages mentioning a universal gathering of God's people. The second parallel passage states,

> Listen, I will tell you a mystery: We will not all sleep, but we will all be changed—in a moment, in the blinking of an eye, at the last trumpet. For the trumpet will sound, and the dead will be raised imperishable, and we will be changed. (1 Cor. 15:51–52)

This passage is in the context of Paul's most descriptive treatment on the resurrection. After a discussion about the resurrection, he shifts his attention to those who will still be alive at Christ's parousia. He says his teaching is a "mystery." Paul does not mean it is a mystery in the sense of keeping his readers in the suspenseful dark. Quite the contrary. He is saying that this revelation has not been previously disclosed by God. What is this new revelation? Paul is teaching that God has ordained that the last generation of the church—those living up to the parousia—will not have to experience death ("we will not all sleep"). Just as the dead will be changed with imperishable, resurrected bodies, the living will also experience this change without having to die. Paul says this will happen at the "last trumpet," which will signal the resurrection and the transformation of those who are alive.

The triad of glorious sounds announces God's parousia purposes. The first purpose is to "awaken" the dead in Christ. The newly resurrected are not caught up to the sky just yet, as we shall see in verse 17. God will apparently use the resurrected on earth as a testimony to the world to proclaim his power over death. This purpose will not be unprecedented, for God displayed his power similarly during his first coming at the death of Christ: "And tombs were opened, and the bodies of many saints who had died were raised. (They came out of the tombs after his resurrection and went into the holy city and appeared to many people)" (Matt. 27:52–53). At Christ's return, how long will the newly resurrected be on earth before the rapture? We are not told exactly, but the text suggests briefly.

Next, verse 17 reads,

> Then we who are alive, who are left, will be suddenly caught up together with them in the clouds to meet the Lord in the air. And so we will always be with the Lord.

The dead in Christ will receive their new bodies first, followed by those who are alive and left at the parousia of Christ. Then at the same time both groups will be caught up in the clouds to meet the Lord in the air. Clouds are a common feature of theophanies accompanying divine presence. It is in those clouds that we meet and experience God's presence in his Son. It is often assumed that the alive will receive their new bodies *as they are being rap-*

tured to the sky. But the text does not state this. Presumably, the alive in their newly transformed bodies will join with the newly resurrected *on earth* as a testimony to the world, then shortly after that union they will be raptured. It should not be assumed that the dead in Christ are raptured before the alive in Christ. The dead in Christ receive their transformed bodies before the alive receive theirs, but both groups—the resurrected and the remnant—will be united *together* on earth before they are raptured at the same time. Most translations indicate this picture, but the Greek text is explicit: *hama* ("together" or "at the same time") *syn* ("with") *autois* ("them") *harpagēsometha* ("snatched away"). Joseph Plevnik summarizes this depiction:

> The first act at the Lord's coming from heaven is that the deceased faithful are brought back to life; then only, once they have been reunited with the living, is everyone taken up by the clouds to meet the Lord. These pointers ["first," "then," "together with"] . . . insist on this sequence of acts. The surviving faithful have no advantage over the deceased: the latter are brought to life, join the living, and are, together with the living, taken up by the clouds.[17]

THE RESURRECTION AND THE RAPTURE

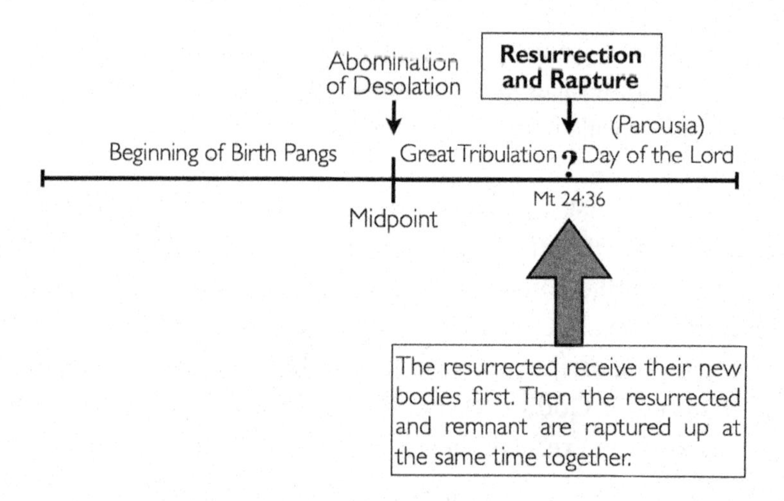

I want to make a few comments on the Greek word *harpazō* that is behind the theological concept of the rapture. This word means "to snatch, take away, seize suddenly." The term *harpazō* is found fourteen times in the New Testament.[18] (To be sure, the term is found in contexts other than the rapture.) It is the word used in verse 17 that underlies our English rendering "suddenly caught [up]." This is where we get the concept of the rapture, which is a word derived from the Latin *rapio*. In the early church, one of the very first translations of the Bible was in Latin, and the translator chose *rapio* as the appropriate Latin verb to translate *harpazō*. Some have denied that the Bible teaches the rapture since the English term is not found in any English translations (even though the term "rapture" would be a very appropriate rendering for an English translation). This surface-level argument is not convincing since the concept of the rapture is clearly taught in verse 17. The lack of the term itself is not unusual because many English theological terms are not found in the Bible while their concepts are found therein (e.g. Trinity, monotheism, inspiration, omniscience, and scores of others).

Four Reasons the Rapture Is in Matthew 24:31

Having examined in depth Paul's teaching on the resurrection and the rapture, this now brings us back to Jesus' teaching on the gathering of the elect.

> "And he will send his angels with a loud trumpet blast, and they will gather his elect from the four winds, from one end of heaven to the other." (Matt. 24:31)

Does the phrase "gather his elect" refer to the rapture? This is a watershed question. It is a vital question because if it does refer to the rapture then the church will face the Antichrist's great tribulation. Jesus ominously warns, "Remember, I have told you ahead of time" (Matt. 24:25). Jesus does not simply say, "Remember, I have told you"; he says, "Remember, I have told you *ahead of time*." It is incumbent upon the student of prophecy to understand not just *that* Jesus is returning, but the *conditions* before his return, especially the crucial event of the Antichrist's persecution. So it is imperative that we examine this matter. The following four reasons support why Matthew 24:31 refers to the rapture.[19]

THE GATHERING OF THE ELECT AS THE RAPTURE

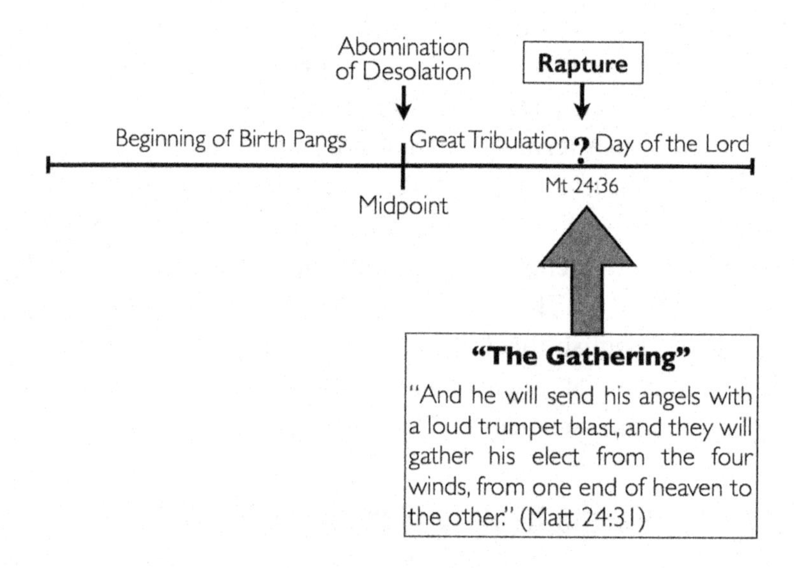

Reason 1: Jesus Uses 'Rapture' Language

In 2 Thessalonians 2:1, Paul writes, "Now regarding the arrival of our Lord Jesus Christ and *our being gathered* [*episynagōgē*] to be with him, we ask you, brothers and sisters . . ." (emphasis mine). Paul is referring to his rapture teaching from 1 Thessalonians 4:17 by using the term *episynagōgē*, meaning an "assembly or gathering." Jesus uses the same term in Matthew 24:31: "And he will send his angels with a loud trumpet blast, and they will gather [*episynagō*] his elect from the four winds, from one end of heaven to the other." Jesus employs the action form of this same word, *episynagō*. To be sure, this is not a technical term for the rapture because it can be used in other contexts; but the point is that it shows that Paul is drawing his teaching from the

Olivet Discourse, using Jesus' own terminology (see the appendix, "Parallels between Jesus and Paul").[20]

Reason 2: Jesus' Use of Daniel on the Resurrection

In Matthew 24:31, the gathering of the elect relates to the resurrection. The book of Daniel was the principle source which Jesus drew for his Olivet Discourse: "So when you see the abomination of desolation—spoken about by Daniel the prophet—standing in the holy place . . . ." (Matt. 24:15). When we employ the principle of interpretation of comparing Scripture with Scripture, we discover that Jesus intends for the gathering in Matthew 24:31 to relate to the resurrection mentioned in Daniel 11:36–12:3, containing a sequence of four key events corresponding to the same sequence in Matthew 24, as the following parallels illustrate:

Daniel 11:36–12:3 Parallels Matthew 24:15–31

The Abomination of Desolation

Daniel: Then the king will do as he pleases. He will exalt and magnify himself above every deity and he will utter presumptuous things against the God of gods. He will succeed until the time of wrath is completed, for what has been decreed must occur. . . . He will pitch his royal tents between the seas toward the beautiful holy mountain. But he will come to his end, with no one to help him (Dan. 11:36, 45).
Olivet Discourse: "So when you see the abomination of desolation—spoken about by Daniel the prophet—standing in the holy place" (Matt. 24:15).

The Great Tribulation

Daniel: There will be a time of distress unlike any other from the nation's beginning up to that time (Dan. 12:1).
Olivet Discourse: "For then there will be great suffering unlike anything that has happened from the beginning of the world until now, or ever will happen" (Matt. 24:21).

Rescue of Elect Remaining

Daniel: But at that time your own people, all those whose names are found written in the book, will escape (Dan. 12:1).
Olivet Discourse: "And if those days had not been cut short, no one would be saved [delivered]. But for the sake of the elect those days will be cut short" (Matt. 24:22).

Resurrection

Daniel: Many of those who sleep in the dusty ground will awake (Dan. 12:2).
Olivet Discourse: "They will gather his elect from the four winds, from one end of heaven to the other" (Matt. 24:31).

This last verse from Daniel 12:2 is considered to be the most explicit reference in the Old Testament to the resurrection: "those who sleep in the dusty ground will awake." Since Jesus explicitly says that he is citing Daniel, and since the sequence of these four events corresponds to Matthew 24, the natural conclusion is that Jesus intends those gathered "from the four winds, from one end of heaven to the other" to refer to the resurrection of God's people. When the disciples sitting on the Mount of Olives heard Jesus refer to the most explicit resurrection passage in the Old Testament, undoubtedly they would have associated "gather his elect" with the resurrection.

Reason 3: Jesus and Paul Address the Inception of the Parousia

No one disagrees that Paul is expounding on the initial aspect of the parousia in 1 Thessalonians 4:15–17, teaching that the resurrection and rapture will happen immediately when Christ comes back. Paul writes, "For we tell you this by the word of the Lord, that we who are alive, who are left *until* the coming of the Lord, will surely not go ahead of those who have fallen asleep" (1 Thess. 4:15, emphasis mine). Notice that Paul states "until" the coming (*parousia*) of the Lord, which addresses the inception of the second coming of Christ. But what about Jesus? Does he also address the inception of the second coming? Jesus describes,

> "For just like the lightning comes from the east and flashes to the west, *so the coming [parousia] of the Son of Man will be.* Wherever the corpse is, there the vultures will gather. Immediately after the suffering of those days, the sun will be darkened, and the moon will not give its light; the stars will fall from heaven, and the powers of heaven will be shaken. *Then the sign* of the Son of Man will appear in heaven, and all the tribes of the earth will mourn. They will see the Son of Man arriving on the clouds of heaven with power and great glory. And he will send his angels with a loud trumpet blast, and they will gather his elect from the four winds, from one end of heaven to the other." (Matt. 24:27–31, emphasis mine)

It is clear from this passage that Jesus is describing the inception of the parousia, not a later transpired stage. First, Jesus gives the sign of the parousia (v. 27), which is the lightning, the Shekinah glory. He teaches that this bright sign will burst through when the natural light goes dark and the "powers of heaven are shaken" (vv. 30–31). Signs are given to announce something; thus, a sign for the inception of the parousia is precisely what Jesus gives in response to his disciples' question. Second, Jesus' parables and similitudes explicitly address the inception of his return (Matt. 24:32–51). His warnings to be watchful would be rendered unintelligible if applied to the end of the day of the Lord's wrath. Third, Jesus states that the parousia will begin "immediately after" the great tribulation (v. 29). The persecution of God's people by the Antichrist will be cut short by the conjunction of the celestial disturbances and the sign of Christ's return, followed by the gathering of his elect.

Jesus and Paul are consistent with describing the beginning stage of the parousia. Jesus' mention of it is brief, while Paul elaborates on it.

INCEPTION OF THE SECOND COMING (PAROUSIA)

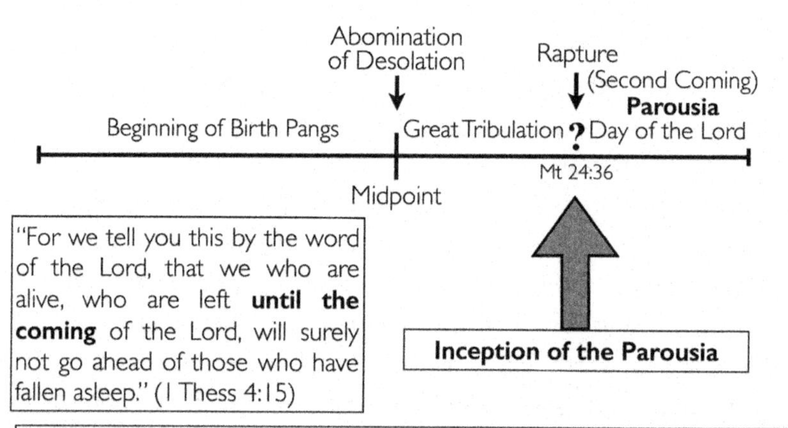

"For just like the lightning comes from the east and flashes to the west, so the **coming** of the Son of Man will be. . . . **Then the sign** of the Son of Man will appear in heaven, and all the tribes of the earth will mourn. They will see the Son of Man arriving on the clouds of heaven with power and great glory." (Matt 24:27, 30)

Reason 4: Gathered 'Out of the Great Tribulation'

In Part 1 we briefly touched on how the elements in Jesus' Olivet Discourse correspond sequentially to Revelation 6. This should not be surprising since Jesus is the source of both. There are seven seals on the scroll that must be opened before the contents of God's wrath are unleashed through the trumpets and bowls. Revelation 6 describes six seals that open sequentially *without interruption.* But before the seventh seal is opened in Revelation 8:1, there is a conspicuous pause in Revelation 7. This interlude between the sixth and seventh seal depicts two groups of people being rescued: 144,000 Jews who are sealed on earth, protecting them from the impending wrath after the seventh seal is opened; and an innumerable crowd in heaven made up of believers from every nation, tribe, people, and language. For our purposes, our attention will be directed to the innumerable crowd in heaven. *Please read Revelation 7:9–17.*

John sees "an enormous crowd that no one could count, made up of persons from every nation, tribe, people, and language." They are depicted as possessing newly resurrected bodies and praising God for their deliverance and resurrection: "dressed in long white robes, and with palm branches in their hands" and having "washed their robes and made them white in the blood of the Lamb." Certainly, the fifth seal martyrs should also be viewed as included with God's people in this picture. "Each of them was given a long white robe and they were told to rest for a little longer" (Rev. 6:11). However, the description "every nation, tribe, people, and language" (7:9) and their robes being washed "white in the blood of the Lamb" (7:14) attests to the description of the church and all of God's people mentioned in Revelation 5:9: "You are worthy to take the scroll and to open its seals because you were killed, and at the cost of your own blood you have purchased for God persons from every tribe, language, people, and nation" (cf. 5:10 with 1:5–6).[21]

This great multitude of believers appearing in heaven confounds John, prompting him to ask, "Who are they and where have they come from?" (Rev. 7:13; cf. Rev. 7:16–17). He is told, "These are the ones who have come out of the great tribulation." This parallels Jesus' teaching that the elect will be gathered out of the great tribulation at his return. "And if those days [the great tribulation] had not been cut short, no one would be saved. But for the sake of the elect those days will be cut short . . . . And he will send his angels with a loud trumpet blast, and they will gather his elect from the four winds, from one end of heaven to the other" (Matt. 24:22, 31; cf. vv. 29–30). This gathering of God's people is also found in Luke's account. "But when these things begin to happen, stand up and raise your heads, because your redemption is drawing near" (Luke 21:28).

This innumerable multitude can be none other than the resurrected and raptured people of God. It is perfectly fitting to see them taken out of the great tribulation with glorified bodies to heaven at this point because it happens just before the seventh seal is opened, triggering the day of the Lord's wrath (Rev. 8:1).

In addition, both accounts in the Olivet Discourse and Revelation 6–7 show that this gathering of God's people happens just after the celestial disturbances (Matt. 24:29–31; Luke 21:25–28; Rev. 6:12–17). In other words, we can say that the fifth seal promises wrath; the sixth seal portends wrath; an interlude in Revelation 7 protects from wrath; and the seventh seal pronounces wrath.

Progression towards God's Wrath	
Seal 5	Promises God's Wrath
Seal 6	Portends God's Wrath
Interlude	Protects from God's Wrath
Seal 7	Pronounces God's Wrath

The parallels between Matthew 24 and Revelation 6–7 are illustrated in the following table.

Matthew 24	**Parallels**	**Revelation 6–7**
4–5	The Antichrist / False christs	First Seal (6:1–2)
6–7	Wars	Second Seal (6:3–4)
7	Famine	Third Seal (6:5–6)
9, 21–22	Martyrdom (Great Tribulation)	Fourth Seal (6:7–8)
9, 21–22	Result of Martyrdom (Great Tribulation)	Fifth Seal (6:9–11)
29	Celestial Disturbances	Sixth Seal (6:12–17)
30–31	Raptured Saints	Interlude (7:9–17)
14, 30, 37–41	Day of the Lord's Wrath	Seventh Seal (Trumpets, Bowls)

I have given four reasons supporting Matthew 24:31 as referring to the rapture. The same language describing Jesus' return is found, not just in Matthew 24, but in Paul's teaching in 2 Thessalonians 2:1. Jesus also draws from Daniel, especially from the most explicit resurrection passage in the Old Testament. In addition, the focus of both Jesus and Paul is on the inception of the second coming. The final reason I gave shows that Jesus and the book of Revelation address the same context and the same sequence of God's people who have "come out of the great tribulation." In my judgment, each reason is compelling, and collectively, they form a cogent defense.

AN OVERVIEW OF THE PREWRATH POSITION

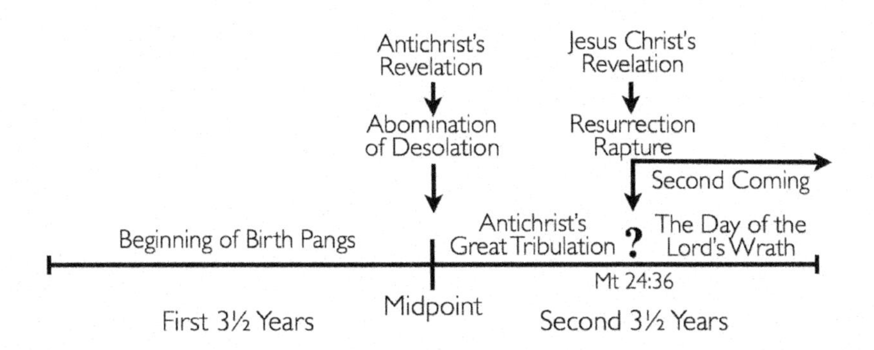

Conclusion

In Part 2, I covered the unique cluster of celestial events that will warn the world of God's impending wrath, as well as function as a signal to the church of their impending deliverance as they suffer during the Antichrist's persecution. Then I considered the teachings on the rapture, concluding with four reasons that the gathering in Matthew 24:31 refers to the rapture. In Part 3, we will consider the next event after the rapture—the day of the Lord's wrath. We will survey the day of the Lord that Jesus knew from selected Old Testament prophets and Paul's important teaching on God's eschatological wrath. I will conclude with the graphic portrayal of the day of the Lord's judgment from the book of Revelation.

PART 3.
The Day of the Lord's Wrath

In our third and final part, I will describe the day of the Lord's wrath. It will be the eschatological period of judgment—dreadful, destructive, and decisive. I will first consider the expression "the day of the Lord." Then I will expound on the day of the Lord that Jesus knew from the Jewish prophets of old. After that, I will concentrate on Paul's main teaching on the day of the Lord, concluding with the book of Revelation's portrayal of the trumpet judgments, bowl judgments, and Armageddon.

The Expression 'the Day of the Lord'

An explanation will acquaint us with the terminology and concept of the day of the Lord. The personal name for God is Yahweh (YHWH), which is the Hebrew behind the word "Lord" in the expression "the day of the Lord." Many English translations render it with small capital letters (Lord), not to give emphasis, but to distinguish God's name from the regular lowercase "Lord," which is the Hebrew term *adonai*. The latter term usually refers to deity or a respectful address. I am keeping it simple. When I use the Old Testament expression "the day of the Lord," you can assume "Lord" is referring to God's name, Yahweh.

The Hebrew term for "day" in this expression is *yôm*. In our context, the term takes on a richer and larger scope than a mere literal twenty-four-hour day. *Yôm* contains about a dozen different meanings in the Old Testament, so context plays an important role. It does refer to a literal twenty-four-hour day when it is associated with a number (e.g. "three days") or other qualifiers such as "full day," "each day," "every day," "a full day," "the Sabbath day," and so on. In contrast, the prophets often used "day" to denote the epochal time when God would break into history in glory and judgment, bringing the ungodly to account. They describe this eschatological period as decisive, yet complex, unfolding over time. The book of Revelation reveals that the fifth trumpet judgment alone will last five months (Rev. 9:5, 10) and the seventh trumpet will unfold for an indeterminate number of days (Rev. 10:7).

To be sure, the "day of the Lord" is not the only biblical expression to refer to God's eschatological judgment upon the ungodly, because the Old and New Testaments use many other expressions (e.g. "that day," "judgment day," "the harvest," "the days of the Son of Man").

All of this judgment discussion about the day of the Lord can give the impression that judgment will be the only characteristic of this day. The same prophets who spoke of eschatological judgment upon the ungodly, however, also prophesied that this "day" would encompass future hope, redemption, and millennial blessings for the righteous (e.g. Isa. 27, 40–66; Mic. 4:6–8; Obad. 15–17; Jer. 30:8–9; Zeph. 3:9–20; Zech. 14). My emphasis on the judgment aspect of this "day" for prewrath purposes is not meant to minimize the importance of the millennial blessings and God's glorious goal to dwell with his people.

The Day of the Lord That Jesus Knew

It should go without saying that there was no "New Testament" during the time of Jesus. The Scriptures that Jesus knew were the

Hebrew Scriptures (the "Old Testament"), also called the Jewish Bible (Tanakh). The Jewish prophets of old that Jesus knew depicted a vivid picture of God's eschatological wrath.

The prophets were privileged ministers who extolled God's holy and faithful attributes, calling Israel back to covenant faithfulness. When Israel did not repent, God vindicated his holiness by judging the rebellious nation. The prophets repeatedly reminded the Israelites of the choice between God's kingdom and human kingdoms—the former characterizing obedience, the latter obstinacy. The prophets pointed to the eventual defeat of human kingdoms to be replaced by the kingdom of peace where God's people would fellowship forever with their Covenant-Creator. But before the kingdom of peace is recreated, the human kingdoms will be purged by God's wrath. This is the consistent message of the prophets, who provide us with a poignant picture. We will look at three of these prophets—Joel, Isaiah, and Zephaniah—who will help us paint this picture of Yahweh's eschatological wrath.

Joel on the Day of the Lord's Wrath

The Bible gives minimal biographical information about this prophet. But it is suggested that he was from the southern kingdom of Judah, possibly even Jerusalem. The chief message in the book of Joel is the day of the Lord, both historical and eschatological. In Joel 1–2:11, a contemporaneous locust plague had invaded Israel, which Joel used to prefigure the near invasion by the Assyrians and Babylonians. He also used it to foreshadow the unparalleled eschatological day of the Lord (2:28–3:21). In response, Joel calls Israel to return to the Lord through repenting of their neglect of the law of God with the hope of heart-contrite repentance (2:12–27). *Please read Joel 2:1–11 for a sober and vivid imagery of the day of the Lord.*

We have already covered Joel's celestial disturbance passage in Part 2, but for completeness' sake, I will mention it again.

> I will produce portents both in the sky and on the earth—blood, fire, and columns of smoke. The sunlight will be turned to darkness and the moon to the color of blood, before the day of the Lord comes—that great and terrible day! (Joel 2:30–31; cf. 3:14–15)

Finally, Joel teaches that the stormy wrath of the day of the Lord will not be limited to unrepentant Israel. The godless nations will endure fiery judgment, as well. This judgment is described in graphic agricultural imagery. *Please read Joel 3:1–2, 12–16 for the graphic agricultural imagery depicting judgment.*

The book of Joel closes with the prophecy of the establishment of God's kingdom, the ultimate goal of the day of the Lord—the Lord shall reign and dwell in Zion (3:17–21).

Joel's description of the day of the Lord reveals it to be characterized by the following:

- Ominous celestial signs
- Dreadful darkness
- Fear and trembling
- Divine decisive judgment
- Presence of a powerful and numerous divine army
- Unprecedented terror
- Fire devouring everything in its path
- Unexpected calamity
- Limited survival

Isaiah on the Day of the Lord's Wrath

Isaiah prophesied during precarious days in the southern kingdom of Judah. His major themes, to name a few, include picturing the Lord as a warrior, redeemer, and a holy sovereign. He warned of impending judgment if the people did not turn back to God in faith and obedience. *Please read Isaiah 2:10–22 for an evocative pronouncement of the day of the Lord.*

The ungodly will not repent when they see the Lord's royal splendor. Instead, they will run from him. This kind of fear does not lead to wisdom. It exposes foolish idolatry. The Lord alone will be exalted in that day, resulting in human humiliation. The world's so-called greatest achievements will no longer be celebrated. The Lord will demolish the eschatological towers of Babel, bringing them to their prideful knees. Self-exalting individuals who worship power, money, entertainment, and other idols will be "brought low." The response from the ungodly contrasts with Isaiah's response to witnessing the Lord's glory a few chapters later when he was given the rare privilege of seeing the Lord in splendid glory in his magnificent throne room. In chapter 6, he describes seeing the Lord of hosts as the seraphim solemnly praise, "Holy, holy, holy is the Lord." Isaiah recognizes his unworthiness and repents of his creaturely sin to purify himself for his prophetic ministry.

In another passage, please read Isaiah 13:6–13 for a portrayal of the ominous countenance of the ungodly. This passage applies to the near judgment on Judah by the Babylonians in 605–586 B.C. (see 13:1); but it also foreshadows the eschatological theophany. Isaiah 13 is a good example of how the prophets often blended the historical with the eschatological. They typically did not demarcate the eschatological with clear temporal indicators, so we have to look to other elements to give us clues. In chapter 13, within this oracle of Babylon, we can discern that parts of it refer to the larger eschatological judgment because of the universal terminology, such as "earth" and "world." In addition, the celestial portents in this passage are strikingly similar to other passages that are clearly in their own eschatological contexts (cf. Joel 2:30–31; Matt. 24:29; Rev. 6:12–13). This passage depicts a holy war compounded by universal catastrophe, a unilateral campaign by the Sovereign Warrior. It will be unabated wrath, resulting in terrified sinners and their destruction. Survival will be "more scarce than pure gold."

Similarly, Isaiah draws from Joel's motif of the celestial disturbances associated with the day of the Lord. There is not only a literal fulfillment in temporal darkness, but there is symbolism in this prophecy, as well. The concept of darkness is fitting since many pagan gods were identified with celestial bodies that give off light, including the moon, stars, and sun. Even today, naturalistic materialism holds that celestial bodies are an end unto themselves, coming into existence, not through a Creator, but through their own supposed self-sustaining power. Accordingly, it will be ironic when God darkens the luminaries to display his own sovereign radiance (cf. Rom. 1:18–32).

The certainty of this day should induce us to examine ourselves for any worldly attachments fettering us from surrendering completely to the Lord of the universe. We should never be too confident, always asking God to search our souls for sin.

For further reading on Isaiah's prophecies concerning God's future judgment and triumph over the earth, I refer the reader to Isaiah 24–27, which has been coined Isaiah's "Little Apocalypse."

Isaiah highlights these elements of the day of the Lord:

- The proud brought low in humiliation
- The ungodly attempting to flee from his judgment
- The Lord alone exalted
- False value of idols exposed
- Foolishness of trusting in human structures
- Utter terror and despair
- God's unabated fury
- Sinners punished
- Celestial darkness
- Unlikely survival

Zephaniah on the Day of the Lord's Wrath

This next prophet furnishes us with a compact yet vivid declaration of the day of the Lord. Zephaniah prophesied to Judah in the seventh century B.C., condemning salient sins such as pagan practices, idolatry, laziness, and pride. *Please read Zephaniah 1:1–3, 14–18 for a portrayal of the day of the Lord as God revealed it to him.*

More than all the other prophets, Zephaniah highlights the universality of God's judgment. "'I will destroy everything from the face of the earth,' says the Lord" (1:2; cf. 3:8). Yahweh is not some mere tribal deity. He rules globally. Zephaniah characterizes this time as fiery wrath, devastation, darkness, and bloodshed for both beasts and humans. The Divine Warrior intrudes definitively into human history. The ungodly have no choice but to submit to his sovereign will. Zephaniah's account of the eschatological intervention has been called the "divine-human collision." Material investments will be impotent to deliver the rebellious in the day of the Lord's angry judgment.

In view of this dreadful picture of wrath, Zephaniah urges repentance and fervent devotion to the Lord (see Zeph. 2:2–3). The prophet closes with hope for a faithful remnant whom God will restore (Zeph. 3:9–20). Only the humble will dwell with God. Thereby, God calls us to repentance and self-examination, exhorting us not to trust in human structures but in submission to his kingdom structures.

Zephaniah characterizes the day of the Lord as follows:

- Fiery wrath
- Devastation and darkness
- Bloodshed of living creatures and humanity
- Submission to God's sovereign judgment
- Impotence of material wealth

Joel, Isaiah, and Zephaniah are three prophets who display a foreboding picture of God's eschatological wrath. However, they are not the last word on what the day of the Lord entails. The progressive revelation given in the New Testament will complete our picture.

Jesus on Back-to-Back Rapture and Wrath

There is a pattern in Scripture of God supernaturally rescuing his people just before he executes divine judgment on the wicked. This is memorably attested to in the story of God's plagues against Egypt, culminating in the deliverance of Israel from the hands of Pharaoh's army that was ultimately destroyed in the Red Sea. This pattern is continued in the context of the eschatological day of the Lord when Paul gives believers the reassuring promise: "For God did not destine us for wrath but for gaining salvation through our Lord Jesus Christ" (1 Thess. 5:9). The term for "salvation" in this verse is *sōtēria*. It has two common meanings: salvation in the sense of physical deliverance and salvation in the sense of non-physical deliverance (such as spiritual salvation). Here it takes on the former meaning since this promise is in the context of the rapture and the day of the Lord; thus, for believers, the day of the Lord will not "overtake you like a thief" (1 Thess. 5:4).

This pattern of deliverance before God's eschatological wrath is especially seen in Jesus' teaching where he emphasizes the back-to-back nature of deliverance and judgment.

> "The days are coming when you will desire to see one of the days of the Son of Man, and you will not see it. Then people will say to you, 'Look, there he is!' or 'Look, here he is!' Do not go out or chase after them. For just like the lightning flashes and lights up the sky from one side to the other, so will the Son of Man be in his day. But first he must suffer many things and be rejected by this generation. Just as it was in the days of Noah, so too it will be in the days of the Son of Man. People were eating, they were drinking, they were marrying, they were being given in marriage—*right up to the day Noah entered the ark*. Then the flood came and destroyed them all." (Luke 17:22–27, emphasis mine; cf. Matt. 24:37–41)

In this passage, there are at least three important truths regarding Christ's return. First, the sign of his second coming will be like lightning that will light up the sky. In Part 2, we covered this in our examination of the Olivet Discourse (Matt. 24:3, 27, 30). This will be his Shekinah glory announcing his divine presence to the entire world. Second, Jesus likens unbelievers at the time of the flood to unbelievers at the time of his second coming. Jesus says people were going on with their everyday affairs of eating, drinking, marrying, and being given in marriage. He does not make reference to gluttony, drunkenness, and immorality. To be sure, the antediluvian world was egregiously God-hating and self-loving (Gen. 6:11–13), and it is safe to assume that they were engaging in gluttony, drunkenness, and immorality (2 Pet. 2:5). But that is not the point Jesus makes here. He is highlighting that they were going on with their everyday activities, indifferent and oblivious of God's coming wrath. In short, the people of Noah's day were unprepared when the flood came. So will it be in the days at the coming of Christ. People will be going on with their everyday business, living only to please themselves. Paul is consistent with this truth, teaching that at the onset of the day of the Lord unbelievers will be saying, "'peace and security,' then sudden destruction comes on them, like labor pains on a pregnant woman, and they will surely not escape" (1 Thess. 5:3). The third point Jesus makes is that this obliviousness occurred "right up to the day" Noah entered the ark. The same day they entered, the flood began, not two days or five days or seven days later. The deluge began the very day Noah and his family entered the ark and shut the door (see Genesis 7:1–18). Noah was told that he had seven days to corral all the animals because "in seven days I will cause it to rain" (Gen. 7:4). At the end of the seven days, "all the fountains of the great deep burst open and the floodgates of the heavens were opened" (Gen. 7:11). This happened "on that very day Noah entered the ark" (Gen. 7:13). There will be no gap of days, weeks, or months between the deliverance of the righteous and the unleashing of God's wrath at his return. It will be back-to-back.

To make sure he is not misunderstood about this truth, Jesus emphasizes this point by citing the episode of Lot and Sodom.

> "Likewise, just as it was in the days of Lot, people were eating, drinking, buying, selling, planting, building; but *on the day* Lot went out from Sodom, fire and sulfur rained down from heaven and destroyed them all. *It will be the same on the day* the Son of Man is revealed. *On that day*, anyone who is on the roof, with his goods in the house, must not come down to take them away, and likewise the person in the field must not turn back. Remember Lot's wife! Whoever tries to keep his life will lose it, but whoever loses his life will preserve it. I tell you, in that night there will be two people in one bed; one will be taken and the other left. There will be two women grinding grain together; one will be taken and the other left." (Luke 17:28–35, emphasis mine)

In the days of Lot—just as in the days of Noah—people were going on with their everyday tasks, "eating, drinking, buying, selling, planting, building." They were unaware and unprepared for God's impending judgment. His judgment began on the same day of Lot's deliverance. "On the day Lot went out from Sodom, fire and sulfur rained down from heaven and destroyed them all" (cf. Gen. 19:23–28). Accordingly, it "will be the same on the day the Son of Man is revealed."

Paul makes this similar point in 2 Thessalonians 1:7: "and to you who are being afflicted to give rest together with us when the Lord Jesus is revealed from heaven with his mighty angels." He instructs that the church will experience affliction right up to the initial day of the revelation of Christ. We know from his previous teaching in his first Thessalonian epistle that this deliverance is the rapture (1 Thess. 4:15–18). In 2 Thessalonians 1:10, he teaches that the exclusion of unbelievers from the presence of the Lord will begin "when he comes to be glorified among his saints and admired on that day among all who have believed." So for believers alive at that time "who believe our testimony" (v. 10), that day will begin eternal rest; but for unbelievers who "do not obey the gospel" (v. 8), it will begin eternal unrest. In other words, there will not be any delay between the rapture of the righteous and the day of the Lord's judgment upon the ungodly. The Lord's coming will be simultaneously twofold.

This "same day" truth contains significant implications because when Scripture teaches that there will be events happening before the day of the Lord, then by necessity these events—the celestial event (Joel 2:30–31), Elijah's coming (Mal. 4:5), and the apostasy and the revelation of the Antichrist (2 Thess. 2:1–4)—will happen before the rapture.

RAPTURE AND THE DAY OF THE LORD: BACK-TO-BACK

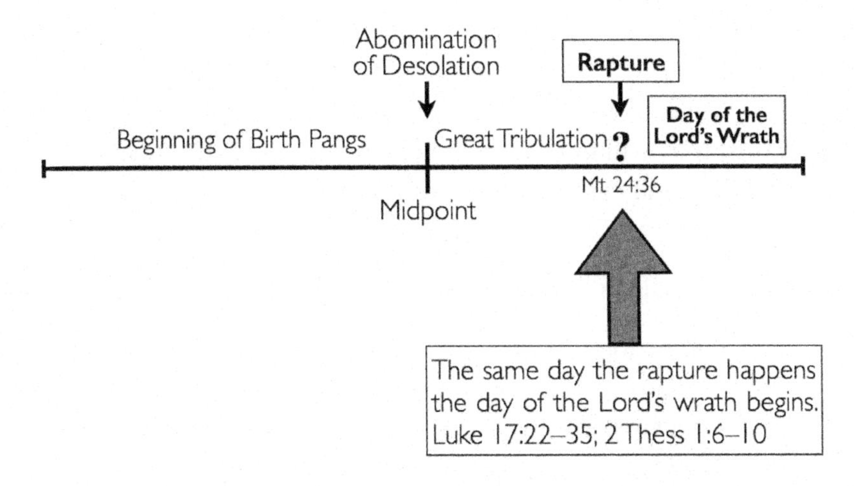

Paul on the Day of the Lord's Wrath

In his first epistle to the Thessalonians, the apostle Paul furnished us with one of the most important biblical teachings on the day of the Lord's wrath.

> Now on the topic of times and seasons, brothers and sisters, you have no need for anything to be written to you. For you know quite well that the day of the Lord will come in the same way as a thief in the night. Now when they are saying, "There is peace and security," then sudden destruction comes on them, like labor pains on a pregnant woman, and they will surely not

> escape. But you, brothers and sisters, are not in the darkness for the day to overtake you like a thief would. (1 Thess. 5:1–4)

In 1 Thessalonians 4:13–18, Paul responded to the hopeless grieving of the Thessalonians by correcting an important point in their eschatology. But that is not the only element in their eschatology causing them to think wrongly. The Thessalonians were feeling trepidation that they might experience divine judgment; accordingly, in 1 Thessalonians 5:1–11, Paul reassures them of God's promise and sovereignty.

In the previous passage on the rapture, Paul comforts the Thessalonian believers about the destiny of their dead loved ones. Now he turns to exhort these same believers about their *own* position in Christ in light of his parousia, teaching them to have spiritual watchfulness. With reference to unbelievers, he explains, they will not be able to escape the sudden return of the Lord—they will experience his eschatological wrath.

Thief-Like Suddenness

> Now on the topic of times and seasons, brothers and sisters, you have no need for anything to be written to you. For you know quite well that the day of the Lord will come in the same way as a thief in the night. (1 Thess. 5:1–2)

Paul's statement "you have no need for anything to be written to you" indicates two things: (1) a question had arisen about the times and seasons of Christ's return, and (2) the Thessalonians had been previously instructed on this matter (e.g. 2 Thess. 2:5). On a surface level, it may be thought that Paul is rebuffing their question about the timing of the Lord's coming, as if they were asking, "Paul, what day is Jesus coming back?" with Paul replying, "I cannot tell you since he is coming back as a thief." This is a careless reading of the context. The Thessalonians are not asking for some specific calendric year-day-hour timing; rather, Paul's answer reveals that they are asking about a *conditional* when. In other words, Paul is teaching that Jesus will come back when a particular condition exists in the world. I will return to this point in a moment.

Paul explains why he does not need to write them about the times and seasons: "for you know quite well that the day of the Lord will come in the same way as a thief in the night." Evidently, Paul used this thief simile at the time he planted the Thessalonian church, but they did not grasp the full implications. The thief simile is frequently used in the New Testament, coined by Christ in his Olivet Discourse (see Matthew 24:43; Luke 12:39–40; cf. 2 Peter 3:10; Revelation 3:3; 16:15). How should we properly understand the intent of this simile? Pretribulationism erroneously imports into this thief imagery the theological system of imminence. But this imagery is not concerned with whether or not prophesied events must happen before Christ's return. Likewise, it is mistaken to read into the thief image the notion of unpredictability since Paul states, "But you, brothers and sisters, are not in the darkness for the day to overtake you like a thief would" (1 Thess. 5:4). Instead, the image conveys a warning for *spiritual readiness.* Paul's point is that if you are not spiritually ready for Christ's return it will come upon you suddenly, with negative consequences. Obedience eliminates the possibility that our Lord will return as a thief to those who are watchful. We belong to Christ; hence we are to live with an attitude of expectancy—spiritual watchfulness. Paul develops this theme, drawing from his thief imagery.

> Now when they are saying, "There is peace and security," then sudden destruction comes on them, like labor pains on a pregnant woman, and they will surely not escape. But you, brothers and sisters, are not in the darkness for the day to overtake you like a thief would. (1 Thess. 5:3–4)

In verse 3, Paul teaches that sudden destruction for the ungodly is the result of the thief-like return of the Lord. He summarizes the perception of unbelievers when they say "peace and security."

During the Antichrist's great tribulation, the world will experience peace and security for those who are loyal to him. Accordingly, Paul prophesies a conditional peace and security that will precede the day of the Lord. This peace and safety, however, will be illusory, a false security for unbelievers, because eventually unforeseen calamity will come upon them just as unexpected labor pains come upon a pregnant woman (cf. Matt. 24:37–39). Paul's analogy of labor pains is drawn from a day-of-the-Lord passage in the Old Testament (Isa. 13:6–10). Since destruction will come suddenly like labor pangs, Paul says the ungodly "will surely not escape" (cf. Luke 21:34–36; Rev. 6:12–17; Isa. 26:17–21).

We should be careful not to confuse Paul's use of the birth pangs analogy with Jesus' purpose in using the same phrasing in the Olivet Discourse ("All these things are the beginning of birth pains," Matt. 24:8). Paul uses the phrase in a completely different application. Jesus applies the birth pangs metaphor to particular events *before* the Antichrist's great tribulation, while Paul applies it to the situation of the onset of the day of the Lord's wrath *after* the great tribulation. Similarly, Jesus uses the birthing metaphor to warn that the end has *not arrived* ("Make sure that you are not alarmed, for this must happen, but the end is still to come. . . . All these things are the beginning of birth pains"). Paul uses it to announce that the end *has arrived* ("then sudden destruction comes on them, like labor pains," 1 Thess. 5:3; cf. Isa. 13:7–8).

STAGES OF BIRTH PANGS

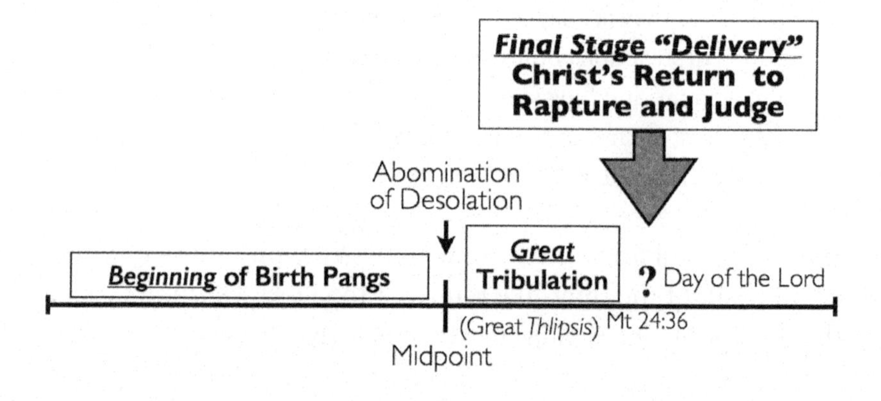

Returning to Paul's passage in verse 4, his reassurance to the Thessalonians implies that they were anxious that they might not escape the day of the Lord. To reassure them, Paul contrasts the ungodly, who will not escape because Christ is coming back as a thief for them, with the obedient-vigilant, who "are not in the darkness for the day to overtake you like a thief would." (This reassuring promise undermines the pretribulational notion that Jesus is secretly coming back as a thief for his church.) The metaphor of darkness refers to being apart from Christ and opposed to God. Conversely, not being in darkness refers to the morality of a child of God; thus by their nature, believers should be spiritually vigilant and prepared.

In summary, the Thessalonians asked about the times and seasons of the day of the Lord. Paul explained that the timing is based on a spiritual condition related through the simile of a thief in the night. The day of the Lord will happen at a particular eschatological point when the ungodly are confidently saying "peace and security," for then there will be sudden destruction. But watchful believers will be ready. Accordingly, 1 Thessalonians 5:1–4 is not teaching that we need to be ready and watchful because the day of the Lord is imminent; instead, Paul is reassuring them that they will not experience the day of the Lord's wrath (cf. 1 Thess. 5:9).

Next, we will shift to our final section of the Bible addressing the day of the Lord's wrath, the book of Revelation. It will introduce us to the systematic elements of judgment that God will execute upon the world.

The Seventh Seal Pronounces Wrath

Jesus is the only one "worthy" (i.e. authorized) to break the seals in order to open the scroll and reclaim his earthly reign through conquering the nations that constitute the kingdom of darkness. The breaking of the seventh and final seal pronounces the day of the Lord's wrath. The opening of the scroll introduces the first phase of God's wrath in a series of trumpet judgments. This will be followed by the second phase, the finale of God's wrath through the seven bowl judgments and Armageddon.

> Now when the Lamb opened the seventh seal there was silence in heaven for about half an hour. Then I saw the seven angels who stand before God, and seven trumpets were given to them. Another angel holding a golden censer came and was stationed at the altar. A large amount of incense was given to him to offer up, with the prayers of all the saints, on the golden altar that is before the throne. The smoke coming from the incense, along with the prayers of the saints, ascended before God from the angel's hand. Then the angel took the censer, filled it with fire from the altar, and threw it on the earth, and there were crashes of thunder, roaring, flashes of lightning, and an earthquake. Now the seven angels holding the seven trumpets prepared to blow them. (Rev. 8:1–6)

Before the first trumpet judgment is sounded, there is a solemn scene in heaven as the seventh seal is opened—a silent overture to the day of the Lord. This is the only place in the book of Revelation that silence is mentioned. From a prewrath perspective, this makes sense. The resurrection and rapture of God's people just occurred (Rev. 7:9–17); now the day of the Lord's wrath is about to be executed. This cosmic moment of silence signals the fearsome wrath of God coming upon the world. The prophet Zephaniah echoes this silence. "Be silent before the Lord God, for the Lord's day of judgment is almost here. The Lord has prepared a sacrificial meal; he has ritually purified his guests" (Zeph. 1:7). And Zechariah writes, "Be silent in the Lord's presence, all people everywhere, for he is being moved to action in his holy dwelling place" (Zech. 2:13; cf. Hab. 2:20). This silence serves God's judicial righteousness. His judgments are true, holy, and blameless—no creature can answer them!

Seven Tormenting Trumpets of God's Wrath

In the Old Testament, trumpets symbolized God's intervention in the lives of his people. In our case, seven angels who stand before God are each given a trumpet. The angels who "stand before God" are a special order of angels. In this context, trumpets symbolize a judgment battle cry. (Incidentally, seven priests blew seven trumpets in the fall of Jericho in Joshua 6:4–9.) We are told that another angel came to the altar with a golden censer. The angel was given much incense "to offer up, with the prayers of all the saints, on the golden altar that is before the throne" (v. 3). The incense offered along with prayers suggests that its purpose was to please God so he would respond. Given this preparatory context for judgment, these soon-to-be-answered prayers most likely include the prayers of the fifth seal martyrs: "How long, Sovereign Master, holy and true, before you judge those who live on the earth and avenge our blood?" (Rev. 6:10).

After the prayers reach God, the silence is broken as "the angel took the censer, filled it with fire from the altar, and threw it on the earth, and there were crashes of thunder, roaring, flashes of lightning, and an earthquake" (Rev. 8:5). These are standard elements of judgment theophany introducing the ensuing trumpet judgments. The censer previously served to offer up incense with the prayers of the saints; now it functions to avenge them. The forceful imagery of throwing fire upon the earth will be repeated in the trumpet judgments (Rev. 8:7–8). A great earthquake occurred at the sixth seal, and here we see another earthquake, with more to come. These earthquakes will remind the ungodly of God's sovereignty over the earth—or shall I say "under the earth"? We will later see this similar theophanic cluster in further instances (Rev. 11:19; 16:18; also 4:5). In short, the hurling of fire, thunder, roaring, lightning, and an earthquake is God's cachet that it is now *his time*. There is no more delay, no more silence. The angels prepare to execute the judgments of God. *Please read Revelation 8:7–9:21 for the account of the trumpet judgments.*

SIX TRUMPETS: FIRST PHASE OF GOD'S WRATH

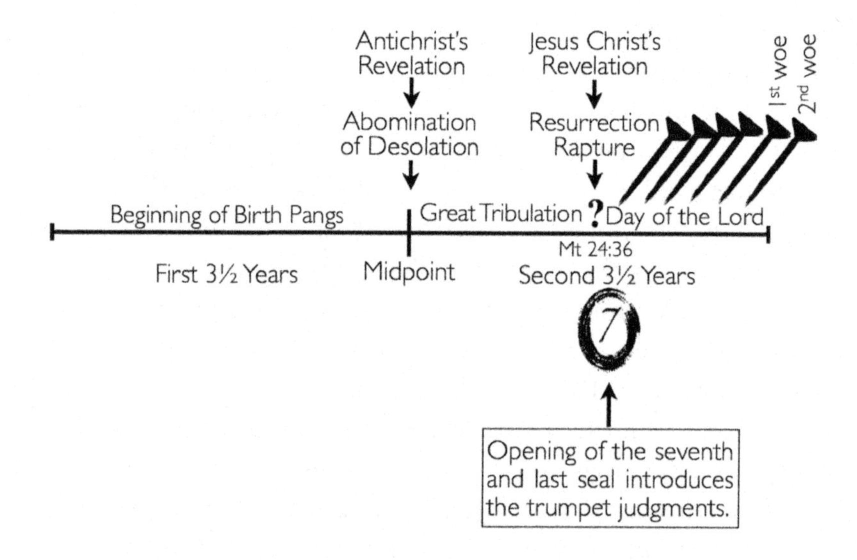

Seven Blitzing Bowls and Battle of Armageddon

We now consider the second phase—the culmination—of the day of the Lord's wrath, which is manifested in the bowl judgments including the battle of Armageddon. This last set of judgments will exterminate what is remaining of the beast's kingdom, reclaiming God's kingdom on earth for Christ's rule.

The completion of the sixth trumpet takes us to the end of the seven-year period, which is then followed by thirty- and forty-five-day periods (cf. Dan. 12:9–13). Soon after the seven-year period is complete, the seventh trumpet will blow, announcing God's reclamation of his reign on earth. The seventh trumpet is the third woe, which marks the highest intensity of the day of the Lord's wrath manifested through the seven bowl judgments. But first is a pronouncement of God's reclamation of his reign on earth.

> The second woe [sixth trumpet] has come and gone; the third is coming quickly. Then the seventh angel blew his trumpet, and there were loud voices in heaven saying: "The kingdom

> of the world has become the kingdom of our Lord and of his Christ, and he will reign for ever and ever." (Rev. 11:14–15; cf. Dan. 2:44)

The "kingdom of the world" is none other than Satan's kingdom manifested through his minion, the Antichrist. The Antichrist will be given 1,260 days of authority to rule the world and persecute God's people (Dan. 7:25; Rev. 13:5). This authority starts at the midpoint of the seven-year period, causing him to commit the abomination of desolation (Dan. 9:27). When his authority expires at the conclusion of the seven-year period, God will formally reclaim his earthly kingdom from Satan at the blowing of the seventh trumpet (Rev. 11:15). During the thirty-day period, the bowl judgments will function to execute the pronouncement of God's kingdom and the demise of the Antichrist's kingdom. The bowls are instrumental in the transitional phase, replacing the Antichrist's rule with Christ's rule.

This transition, however, will not go unopposed by the Antichrist. He will refuse to accept Jesus' authority as king at the seventh-trumpet pronouncement. The Antichrist is not going to raise the white flag and hand over his kingdom just like that. After his authority of 1,260 days expires, he will attempt (unsuccessfully) to keep his authority, kingdom, and followers by waging war against Christ. He is going to fight it out, even though his divinely given authority has expired. The first act of King Jesus, therefore, is to preemptively strike and wipe out his enemies who oppose his kingdom through the bowl judgments and the battle of Armageddon, where the Antichrist's ultimate destruction is realized (Rev. 19:20).

The trumpet judgments require a substantive time to unfold; for example, the fifth trumpet lasts five months (Rev. 9:5, 10). In contrast, the nature and purpose of the bowl judgments will unfold rapidly during the thirty days that follow the seven-year period. The prophet Daniel provides evidence of this additional thirty-day period following the seven-year period. The abomination of desolation will last thirty additional days after the completion of the Antichrist's authority of 1,260 days. "From the time that the daily sacrifice is removed and the abomination that causes desolation is set in place, there are 1,290 days [an additional thirty days]" (Dan. 12:11). At the completion of this thirty-day period, the end of the desolation will coincide with the destruction of the desolator (the Antichrist).

> And he [the Antichrist] will make a firm covenant with the many for one week [seven years], but in the middle of the week he will put a stop to sacrifice and grain offering; and on the wing of abominations will come one who makes desolate [the Antichrist], even *until a complete destruction, one that is decreed, is poured out on the one who makes desolate* [the Antichrist] (Dan. 9:27 NASB, emphasis mine).

This destruction of the desolator-Antichrist is depicted in the aftermath of Armageddon when he is thrown alive in the lake of fire (Rev. 19:20). Accordingly, the bowls, including the battle of Armageddon, will unfold during the brief thirty-day period.

The briefness of God's final wrath is also conveyed in the use of the imagery of the bowls. The New Testament mentions at least fifteen different jars, bowls, baskets, and other types of vessels. However, the term for this particular "bowl" is *phialē*, which means a "broad, shallow bowl."[22] This choice of imagery is not arbitrary but connotes swift judgment. It suggests that emptying the contents of God's final wrath will happen swiftly. This imagery evokes a salvo of bowl judgments emptied until they are completed, like a grand finale to a fireworks display. Thus, it fits well for the brief thirty-day period.

The sixth bowl is unique from the other bowl judgments because there is no expressed wrath. However, it describes the preparation for God's climactic battle-judgment on the nations and the beast's kingdom. There is irony in this preparation. Demonic forces will draw the kings of the earth together, but the battle is not so much a battle as it is a divine summons for the nations to come and receive their judgment.

This sixth bowl reveals the notorious apocalyptic location for the battle where the nations' armies will gather and eventually be defeated by the Lord and his holy armies. "Now the spirits gathered the kings and their armies to the place that is called Armageddon in Hebrew" (Rev. 16:16). The New American Standard Bible renders this as "Har-magedon" (*Harmagedōn*)." The common English spelling is "Armageddon," and it is mentioned once in all of Scripture. What is the meaning of "Armageddon" (*Harmagedōn*)? In my judgment, the best understanding is in the literal sense, the Mount of Megiddo. There was a city on a hill by the name Megiddo in Palestine overlooking the Valley of Jezreel, which is also called the Valley of Megiddo.[23] *Please read Revelation 15:1–16:21; 19:11–21 for the account of the bowl judgments and the Battle of Armageddon.*

POST SEVEN-YEAR PERIOD

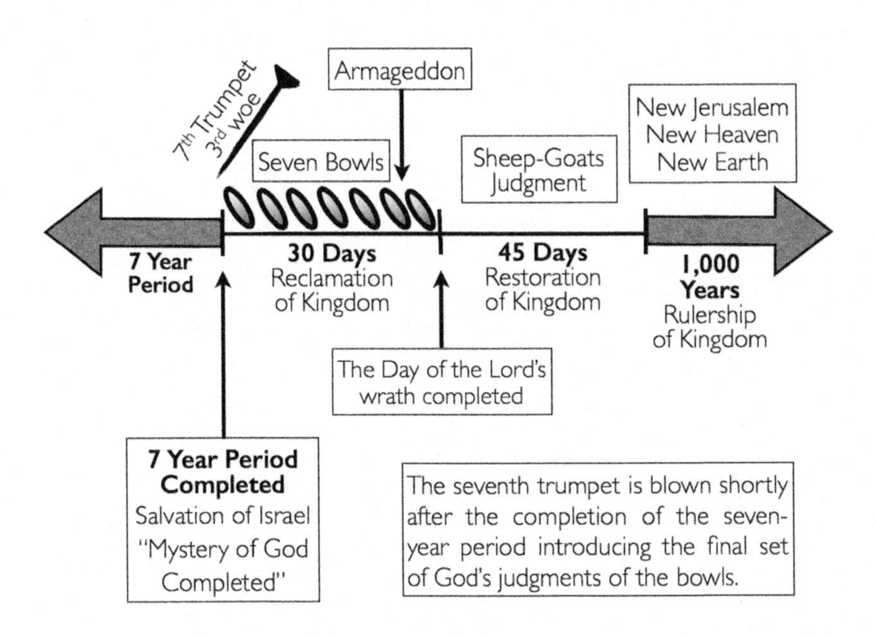

Conclusion

In Part 3, I started with explaining the expression "the day of the Lord." Then I considered the day of the Lord that Jesus knew from the Jewish prophets, followed by Jesus' teaching that the rapture will happen on the same day that the day of the Lord's wrath begins. Next I focused on the apostle Paul's teaching of the day of the Lord, concluding with the book of Revelation's portrayal of the systematic judgments.

We have concluded our study on the second coming of Christ. In Luke 18:8 Jesus asks the question, "When the Son of Man comes, will he find faith on earth?" Jesus' ominous question implies that there will be a temptation to apostatize. In his Olivet Discourse, Jesus warns that there will be concrete temptations facing believers during the great tribulation, including persecution, deception, and slothfulness. It is imperative that we prepare our hearts to be "overcomers" for what may soon come to pass. This is why Jesus warns, "Remember, I have told you ahead of time" (Matt. 24:25).

Appendix 1. Parallels between Jesus and Paul

There are thirty parallels between Jesus' teaching on the second coming in the Olivet Discourse and Paul's teaching on the second coming in the Thessalonian letters. This comparison of Scripture with Scripture shows Paul's dependence on the Olivet Discourse. We should not be surprised by these parallels since Paul explicitly claims dependence on Jesus: "by the word of the Lord" (1 Thess. 4:15). This demonstrates that Jesus intended the Olivet Discourse to be a teaching for *the church*. It is profoundly mistaken to dismiss Jesus' warnings in the Olivet Discourse for the church today, making them applicable only to believers who lived in A.D. 70 (preterism) or to Jewish believers who will live during the "tribulation" (pretribulationism). See the following page for the table of parallels.

Jesus Matt. 24–25	Parallels on the Second Coming	Paul I & II Thess.
24:3–4	Christ is the Source	I.4:15
24:3, 27, 37, 39	Context: The Parousia	I.4:15; II.2:1, 8
24:4–5, 23–26	Do Not Be Deceived	II.2:3
24:6	Alarmed the End Has Come	II.2:2
24:15	Antichrist's Desolation	II.2.4
24:21–22	Opposition By Antichrist	II.2:3–4, 8–9
24:24	Deceiving Signs and Wonders	II.2:9–10
24:24	Elect Will Not Be Deceived	II.2:9–14
24:12	Lawlessness	II.2:3, 12
24:10–11	Apostasy of Many	II.2:3
24:13, 22, 31, 40–41 (Lk 21:28)	Surviving Believers Delivered	I.4:15, 17; 5:9; II.1:7
24:22, 29–31	Persecution Cut Short	II.1:6–7; 2:8
24:27, 30	Initiation of the Parousia	I.4:15, II.2:1, 8
24:29–30	Parousia Follows Antichrist	II.2:8
24:27–30	Universal Perception	I.4:16; II.1:7–8
24:30	Jesus with Clouds	I.4:17
24:30	Power and Glory	II.1:9
24:31	Angelic Presence	I.4:16; II.1:7
24:31	Trumpet Call	I.4:16
24:31	Gathering	I.4:17; II.2:1
25:6	Meeting (*Apantēsis*)	I.4:17
24:37–41 (Lk 17:22–35)	Back-to-Back Rapture & Wrath	II.1:6–10
24:37–41	"Peace and Safety"	I.5:3
24:43	Thief in the Night	I.5:2, 4
24:37–41 (Lk 21:34)	Sudden Destruction for Ungodly	I.5:2–3
24:29–30, 37–39	Initiation of the Day of the Lord	I.5:1–3, II.1:7–8
25:10–13 (Lk 21:36)	Inescapable for the Unprepared	I.5:3
24:32–33	Knowing the Season	I.5:1
24:45–46	The Faithful at His Coming	I.5:4–5, 8
24:42–25:13 (Lk 21:34–36)	Be Watchful and Expectant	I.5:6–8

Appendix 2. Proposed Structure to the Book of Revelation

A common area of disagreement with respect to the book of Revelation is the structure of the book. There is, however, consensus on a basic formal structure. Most agree that the prologue is found in Revelation 1:1–8 or 1:1–20 and the epilogue in 22:6–21. There is also widespread agreement that the letters to the seven churches in chapters 2–3 contain a discernible section. So we are left with the body in Revelation 4:1–22:5. There have been several valid proposals regarding its structure.

Some have structured it by seeing a *temporal* nature from John's perspective. "Therefore write what you saw, what is, and what will be after these things" (Rev. 1:19). Another common arrangement is the *literary* nature in which John is summoned three times to witness sets of new visions (4:1–16:21; 17:1–21:8; 21:9–22:5). Some prefer to view Revelation principally through the lens of a *kingdom* division in which the first half (1–11) narrates events unfolding up to God's reclamation of his kingdom and defeat of Satan's: "The kingdom of the world has become the kingdom of our Lord and of his Christ, and he will reign for ever and ever" (Rev. 11:15). The second half (12–22) is understood as restating these events by expanding or fleshing them out. Finally, the most conspicuous structure John gives is the *septet* (set of seven) arrangement, with five series of sevens, or septets. The first septet is the letters to the seven churches (2–3). The second is a scroll sealed with seven seals (6:1–17; 8:1). The third is the trumpet judgments (8:2–9:21; 11:15–19). The fourth is the bowls, which are said to contain God's final wrath (15:1–16:21). The fifth septet—the only one not explicitly enumerated—is seven visions that share similar features with each other (12–14).

Another literary phenomenon in the book that is very important but sometimes minimized is the use of parentheses. Parentheses function as pauses in the narrative to provide development on previous events before moving forward again. There are minor parenthetical passages scattered throughout the book and two major parenthetical passages (12–14; 17:1–20:3). The first half of the book, chapters 1–11, is naturally sequential, taking us up to the completion of the seven-year period. Following this is the first major parenthetical section in chapters 12–14, giving a panoramic view of the kingdom conflict between Satan and God. The section spans the period of the Messianic promise during Israel's history, then focuses mostly on the Antichrist's great tribulation and concludes with the eschatological harvests of deliverance and judgment at Christ's coming.[24] The narrative picks up at Revelation 15–16 with the bowl judgments. The second major parenthetical section is found in chapters 17:1–20:3. This section develops a few key events, including the sixth and seventh bowls, the great prostitute and the beast's authority, the destruction of the great city of "Babylon," God being glorified from heaven, the marriage supper of the Lamb, and the defeat of the "three adversaries of God." Finally, the conclusion to the book highlights the beginning of the millennium in chapters 20:4–22:21.

I want to make a couple of remarks about the first major parenthetical section found in Revelation 12–14 so we might properly interpret it in light of the overall structure in the book. First, we cannot force every chapter into a chronological fashion; otherwise, we will find ourselves confounded by conflicting events, especially with the events described in this section. To be sure, the narrative does exhibit a *general-progressive* movement. For example, we know that the climax in chapters 19–22 follows the narrative in chapters 1–18; and it is self-evident that chapters 6–22 follow chapters 1–5. Even though the narrative chapters of the seals, trumpets, and bowls are sequential, chapters 12–14 are peculiar in that they do not chronologically follow the narrative in chapters 8–11. For example, references in chapters 12–14 depict the beginning of the Antichrist's campaign, while the narrative in chapters 8–9 describes the trumpet judgments. But we know that God's wrath does not begin *before* the persecution of the Antichrist. So how does the interpreter account for this exception to an otherwise sequential narrative? The question of the chronology of chapters 12–14 is resolved when interpreters recognize that these chapters function as a parenthetical unit containing seven visions. They serve to pause the narrative to give development on previous events that happened mostly during the seven-year period before picking up again in chapters 15–16, which describe the bowl judgments that will occur immediately after the seven-year period.

The literary device of parentheses is not unique to Revelation. It is also found in two other eschatological passages: Matthew 24 and Daniel 7. Matthew 24:9–14 is an overview of the great tribulation, while verses 15–28 are parenthetical, developing the great tribulation. Daniel 7:1–14 is a narrative overview followed by a parenthetical development of the fourth beast in verses 15–27.

A "forest picture" of the book of Revelation will be helpful since it is easy to become lost within the trees of the verses. See the following page for my proposed structure to the book of Revelation.

PROLOGUE AND RECIPIENTS

1. Prologue

2–3. The Seven Churches

BEFORE THE DAY OF THE LORD

4. A Vision of Heavenly Worship
5. The Seven-Sealed Scroll and the Worthy Lamb
6. Opening the Six Seals
7. Protected: 144,000 Jews Sealed and an Innumerable Multitude Delivered

THE DAY OF THE LORD

8. Seventh Seal Opened: First Four Trumpet Judgments
9. Fifth Trumpet / First Woe; Sixth Trumpet / Second Woe

SEVEN-YEAR PERIOD COMPLETED

10. Mighty Angel and the Mystery of God Completed

11:1–13. Completion of Ministry of the Two Witnesses

11:14–19. Seventh Trumpet / Third Woe and God's Kingdom Reclaimed

PARENTHESIS 1: COSMIC CONFLICT

12. Panorama of Satan's Schemes
13. Loyalty to the Antichrist or Jesus Christ?
14. Redeemed 144,000 Jews; Impending Judgments; Harvests of the Earth

THE DAY OF THE LORD COMPLETED

15. Prelude to the Bowl Judgments
16. Seventh Trumpet / Third Woe Continued in the Seven Bowl Judgments

PARENTHESIS 2: THE FALL OF BABYLON AND ANTICHRIST

17. The Great Prostitute and the Beast's Authority
18. Destruction of the Great City of "Babylon"

19:1–10. God Glorified from Heaven; Marriage Supper of the Lamb
19:11–20:3. Defeat of the "Three Adversaries of God"

BEGINNING OF THE MILLENNIUM AND RENEWAL

20:4–6. Types of Resurrection
20:7–15. Satan and the Ungodly Perish
21:1–22:5. New Heaven, New Earth, New Jerusalem
22:6–21. Epilogue

Appendix 3. Expectancy, Not Imminency

Since the day of the Lord's wrath begins on the very same day that God delivers the righteous (Luke 17:22–35; 2 Thess. 1:6–10), this has ramifications for the pretribulational teaching that Christ may rapture the church at any moment (i.e. imminency). Imminency means that there cannot be any prophesied events that *must* occur before the rapture. Pretribulationists argue that if the Bible predicts an event happening before the rapture, then Christ's return can no longer be imminent. But does the Bible teach imminency? Scripture gives four explicit prophesied events that must occur before the day of the Lord. Given this same-day teaching of rapture and wrath, by necessity these events will occur before the rapture. We have already discussed the celestial disturbance event, but it would be good to note it again here.

> I will produce portents both in the sky and on the earth—blood, fire, and columns of smoke. The sunlight will be turned to darkness and the moon to the color of blood, before the day of the Lord comes—that great and terrible day! (Joel 2:30–31)

A second Old Testament prophet, Malachi, foretold another event that would take place before the day of the Lord. "Look, I will send you Elijah the prophet *before* the great and terrible day of the Lord arrives" (Mal. 4:5, emphasis mine). John the Baptist was a type or pattern of Elijah, but he was not the fulfillment of his future ministry.

Turning to the New Testament, we have also covered the apostle Paul's teaching, but we will comment on it again. He furnishes us with two more prophetic events that will occur before the day of the Lord (and thereby before the rapture). He writes,

> Now concerning the coming of our Lord Jesus Christ and our being gathered together to him, we ask you, brothers, not to be quickly shaken in mind or alarmed, either by a spirit or a spoken word, or a letter seeming to be from us, to the effect that the day of the Lord has come. Let no one deceive you in any way. For that day will not come, unless the rebellion comes first, and the man of lawlessness is revealed, the son of destruction, who opposes and exalts himself against every so-called god or object of worship, so that he takes his seat in the temple of God, proclaiming himself to be God. (2 Thess. 2:1–4 ESV)

In this passage, it is noteworthy that Paul gives the rapture ("gathered together to him") a close connection to the day of the Lord. This is because in the immediate context he explains that the wrath of God begins on the same day as God's people are delivered from their persecution (2 Thess. 1:6–10). He then gives two discernible events that must occur before the day of the Lord begins, reassuring the Thessalonian believers that the day of the Lord's wrath has not yet occurred: (1) "the rebellion" (i.e. a well-known apostasy that will take place), and (2) the "man of lawlessness" (i.e. the Antichrist) will be revealed, who will take "his seat in the temple of God, proclaiming himself to be God."

Thus, instead of imminency, the Bible teaches *expectancy* for our Lord's return. The New Testament writers address their contemporary believers as if the second coming of Christ could happen in their generation, but not before key prophetic events would take place: the celestial disturbances, the coming of Elijah, the apostasy, and the Antichrist's revelation.[25] It is possible that our generation of the church could be the one that witnesses these events. Time will tell. In the meantime, we must be watchful, obedient, and faithful to our Lord, lest he comes back at a time in our life when we are not spiritually ready to meet him.

EXPECTANCY—NOT IMMINENCY

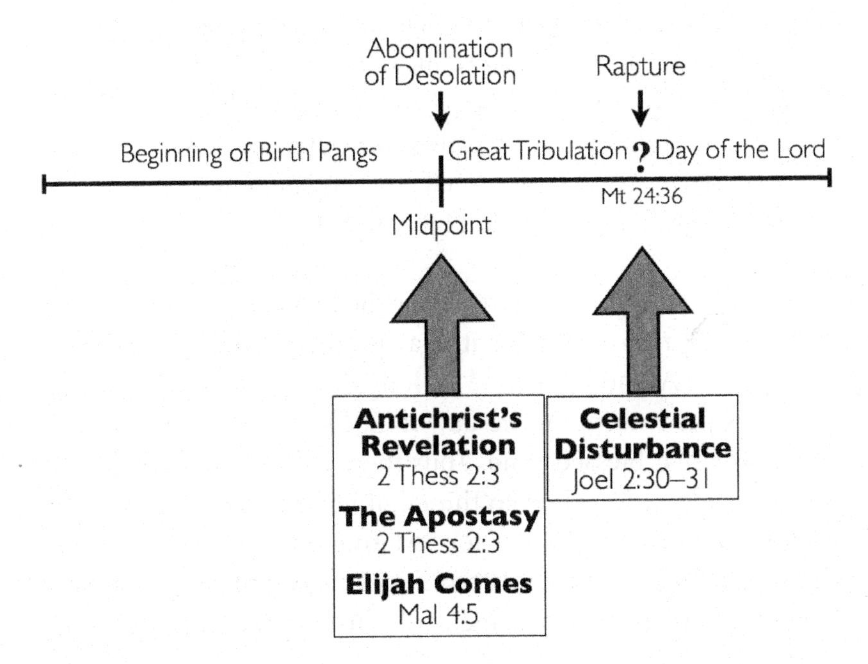

Next, I want to briefly respond to the pretribulational proof text of Titus 2:13: "waiting for our blessed hope, the appearing of the glory of our great God and Savior Jesus Christ" (ESV). This verse is used as a proof text, but it contains no hint of imminency. The verse simply teaches that our blessed hope is the "appearing of the glory of our great God and Savior Jesus Christ." Pretribulationism teaches that the return of Jesus can no longer be a blessed hope if prophetic events must occur before the rapture. But why not? Logically, that makes no sense. I can look forward to the blessed time when the spring flowers bloom, but before that happens the snow must first melt. And I can look forward to being a parent, but a couple of things must happen first unless a stork imminently comes along!

Saying that the rapture cannot be a blessed hope if there are prophesied events that must come first makes no biblical sense either. For example, Peter writes,

> Since all these things are thus to be dissolved, what sort of people ought you to be in lives of holiness and godliness, waiting for and hastening the coming of the day of God, because of which the heavens will be set on fire and dissolved, and the heavenly bodies will melt as they burn! But according to his promise we are waiting for new heavens and a new earth in which righteousness dwells. (2 Pet. 3:11–13 ESV)

Peter teaches that we are to wait for the blessed time of the new heavens and new earth, for it is a "promise" when "righteousness dwells." At the same time we long for that blessed age, Peter describes the coming of the day of God's wrath that must happen *before* that blessed time. Thus there is biblical precedent to long for a blessed time, even though it will be preceded by other events. Moreover, the term for "waiting" in Titus 2:13 ("waiting for our blessed hope") is *prosdechomai*, which simply means "look forward to the fulfillment of our expectation." The term never means "imminence."

Another objection I have heard not a few times is that the blessed hope of Christ's return cannot be blessed if the church has to go through the Antichrist's great tribulation before the rapture. A version of this goes something like this: "I am looking for the true Christ, not the Antichrist!" This sounds pious at first, but there is no biblical substance behind it. In contrast, Peter instructs the church that persecution will be the norm occurring right up to the return of Christ.

> Beloved, do not be surprised at the fiery trial when it comes upon you to test you, as though something strange were happening to you. But rejoice insofar as you share Christ's sufferings, that you may also rejoice and be glad when his glory is revealed. (1 Pet. 4:12–13 ESV)

Not only does Peter teach that the revelation of Christ will be a time of rejoicing, but he teaches that the persecution that occurs just beforehand will make that return *all the more* blessed. For Peter, knowing difficult times are coming should intensify our blessed hope to be with the Lord, not diminish it. In short, Peter and Paul speak of the *doxa*, the glory, of his revelation/appearing, which will be a time of blessed rejoicing.

Here is something else to consider. For which group of believers do you think the return of Christ will be considered more blessed: complacent believers fixed on their couches, watching television and filling their stomachs full of food? Or believers who live in a persecuted country fasting and trusting God during the threat of imprisonment? I think the answer is obvious. The Antichrist's great tribulation will refine the faith of believers and galvanize eager anticipation to be with their Rescuer-Groom. The blessed hope is not a secret, imminent rapture. It is simply seeing and being with our Savior in our glorified state at his revelation. "[W]aiting for our blessed hope, the appearing of the glory of our great God and Savior Jesus Christ" (Titus 2:13 ESV). The great tribulation will heighten that hope.

Pretribulational imminency is a relatively new British-American teaching in church history, originating in the nineteenth century by the Plymouth Brethren theologian John Nelson Darby. If it is found in other parts of the world today, it is only because it has been exported by American and British pretribulational missionaries. In contrast, while the "prewrath" label and teaching was developed a few decades ago, the essence of prewrath teaching reaches back to the early church period. By essence, I mean the key issue that the church will encounter the persecution of the Antichrist. To be sure, not every early church writer in the first two centuries wrote on this subject. But each one who did address it, wrote in a consistent, singular voice affirming that the church would face the Antichrist. The pretribulational teaching cannot attest to this antiquity. Instead, it took more than seventeen hundred years before someone came along to introduce the pretribulational concept of a so-called imminent rapture of the church that would happen before the Antichrist's arrival.[26]

It is wise to learn from those who have gone before us, since church history can teach us a lot. Our final authority, however, is the Word of God, and that is where we must find inspired teaching for faith and practice. For some this matter that the Bible does not teach imminency, but rather expectancy, may be new, even challenging. You might have grown up in a tradition that assumed the imminency of the Lord's return. If this describes you, I encourage you to be a "Berean" in the faith and test everything with the Word of God. "These [Bereans] were more open-minded than those in Thessalonica, for they eagerly received the message, examining the scriptures carefully every day to see if these things were so" (Acts 17:11).

Notes

1. See Harold W. Hoehner, *Chronological Aspects of the Life of Christ* (Grand Rapids: Zondervan, 1977), 115–39.

2. The verb *gābar* is in the Hebrew hiphil stem, which expresses causative action. Ludwig Koehler and Walter Baumgartner, *The Hebrew and Aramaic Lexicon of the Old Testament,* electronic ed., trans. and ed. M. E. J. Richardson (Leiden: Brill, 2000); cf. J. G. Baldwin, *Daniel* (Downers Grove: InterVarsity, 1978), 171.

3. Throughout this book, unless otherwise noted, Greek definitions will be from *A Greek-English Lexicon of the New Testament and Other Early Christian Literature*, rev. and ed. Fredrick W. Danker, 3rd ed. (Chicago: University of Chicago Press, 2000).

4. Daniel Wallace, *Greek Grammar Beyond the Basics: An Exegetical Syntax of the New Testament* (Grand Rapids: Zondervan, 1996), 673. However, it is possible *oun* can sometimes indicate a "transition to something new." But in our context, there is no evidence of this because the narrative clearly shows that *oun* functions to show result or inference of the spiritual action the disciples are to take from the persecution in verses 9–14; in addition, starting with verse 15, *oun* develops the agent and nature of the persecution.

5. In Greek grammatical terminology, the article in this context likely indicates a "well-known" sense. Daniel Wallace comments on this particular category, "The ['well-known'] article points out an object that is well known." *Greek Grammar Beyond the Basics*, 225. But this article could have an anaphoric sense, denoting a previous reference, since Paul states, "Surely you recall that I used to tell you these things while I was still with you" (2 Thess. 2:5). But the anaphoric article is broader than the well-known article and thus could include the well-known sense as well. The question Wallace says we must ask is, "*Why* is it well known?" *Greek Grammar Beyond the Basics*, 222. If the apostasy is caused by the Antichrist's great tribulation (as I will argue above), then it could be the most significant (worst) case of apostasy in Jewish or Christian history.

6. It is often assumed by some interpreters that in order to fulfill this prophecy a colossal Solomonic-like temple complex must be rebuilt. This is not the case. The term for "temple" in verse 4 is *naos*, which does not require a large temple-complex. It can refer to something much simpler, such as a tent-like structure or the inner sanctuary. Such a structure could be erected in a matter of weeks, or less.

7. Over the centuries, various theories have been propounded attempting to identify the restrainer. To name a few: the Holy Spirit, God the Father, the universal church, government, the Roman Empire, and the preaching of the gospel. And there are interpreters who have thrown up their hands and claimed an impasse to the restrainer quest. Recently, however, there has been groundbreaking research on this topic by Thessalonian scholar Colin R. Nicholl. He contends that the restrainer is Michael the Archangel, whose ministry ceases and causes the eschatological temple to be desolated by the Antichrist, an event that is ensued by the Antichrist's great tribulation against God's people. For an outline of his arguments, see *Antichrist Before the Day of the Lord*, 38–9. See also Nicholl's important article "Michael, The Restrainer Removed (2 Thess. 2:6–7)," *Journal of Theological Studies* 51 (2000): 27–53. A few years later he included this article in

his important work on the Thessalonian epistles, *From Hope to Despair in Thessalonica: Situating 1 and 2 Thessalonians*, Society for New Testament Studies Monograph Series 126 (Cambridge: Cambridge University Press, 2004).

8. George Eldon Ladd, *The Blessed Hope: A Biblical Study of the Second Advent and the Rapture* (Grand Rapids: Eerdmans, 1956), 6–7.

9. For my biblical support on this point, see *Antichrist Before the Day of the Lord*, 211–4.

10. G. K. Beale, *The Book of Revelation: A Commentary on the Greek Text* (Grand Rapids: Eerdmans, 1999), 381.

11. The Greek construction suggests that "the beasts" refers to the Antichrist and his religious accomplice. The first three entities, "sword, famine, and pestilence," are functioning as "dative of means/instrument." The fourth entity, "the beasts," is functioning as the "ultimate agent," or, more probable in this context, the "intermediate agent," with the ultimate agent being Death and Hades. In other words, this indicates that the beasts are agents themselves and may be using the sword, famine, and pestilence as means to achieve an end. The text reads, "*apokteinai* [to kill] *en rhomphaia* [with sword] *kai en limō* [and with famine] *kai en thanatō* [and with pestilence] *kai hypo tōn thērion tēs gēs* [and by the wild beasts of the earth]." The first three prepositional phrases that have *en* plus the dative indicate "means/instrument." The last prepositional phrase *hypo* plus the genitive indicates the "ultimate agent" (or possibly an intermediate agent). Wallace, *Greek Grammar Beyond the Basics*, 431–5. This is consistent with the fact that it will be Satan who will possess the Antichrist (see 2 Thess. 2:5–10; Rev. 13). And we know it will be the Antichrist who will kill believers by the "sword" and prevent anyone from buying food if they do not possess his mark (Rev. 13:4–10; 20:4).

12. In Greek grammatical terminology, the article in this context likely indicates a "well-known" sense. Wallace, *Greek Grammar Beyond the Basics*, 225. Another category of the article this example may fall into is the "kataphoric article." Wallace explains this second category: "The first mention, with the article,

is anticipatory, followed by a phrase or statement that defines or qualifies the thing mentioned." *Greek Grammar Beyond the Basics*, 220. In this case, the beasts are qualified as those "of the earth" (cf. Rev. 13:11; Dan. 7:17).

13. Occasionally, I hear pretribulational proponents mistakenly describe prewrath as teaching that the rapture will occur three-quarters into the seven-year period. This is a gross misrepresentation. Prewrath teaches that the rapture will occur *sometime during the second half of the seven-year period.* It does not teach any specificity as to the timing of the rapture such as "three-quarters."

14. Johannes P. Louw and Eugene A. Nida, eds., *Greek-English Lexicon of the New Testament Based on Semantic Domains*, 2nd ed., electronic ed. (New York: United Bible Societies, 1989).

15. Ceslas Spicq, *Theological Lexicon of the New Testament*, electronic ed., trans. and ed. James D. Ernest (Peabody: Hendrickson, 1994).

16. I want to clear up a common assumption. It has erroneously been assumed by many that the second coming begins with the battle of Armageddon. The biblical evidence, however, shows that the parousia begins with Christ's appearance in the clouds to deliver his people, followed by the day of the Lord's wrath executed through the trumpet judgments, and then followed by the bowl judgments and Armageddon. At the rapture, the souls of believers who have died come with Christ to *receive* their new bodies. It is a deliverance event (1 Thess. 4:14). In contrast, at Armageddon, the resurrected believers come with Christ *already in* their new bodies. It is a judgment event. "The armies that are in heaven, *dressed in white, clean, fine linen,* were following him on white horses" (Rev. 19:14, emphasis mine). We know that these armies are believers because we are told a few verses earlier that it is the bride (i.e. believers): "'Let us rejoice and exult and give him glory, because the wedding celebration of the Lamb has come, and his bride has made herself ready. She was permitted to be dressed in *bright, clean, fine linen*' (*for the fine linen is the righteous deeds of the saints*)" (Rev. 19:7–8, emphasis mine). In

one instance in Revelation, angels are depicted wearing similar attire (Rev. 15:6), while saints are seen wearing white in multiple instances (Rev. 3:4–5, 18; 6:11; 7:9, 13–14; 19:7–8). The context of the redemptive marriage supper joins the bride with the Lamb; and we see the bride and the Lamb going to battle against their enemies, resulting in a judgment supper: "Then I saw an angel standing in the sun, and with a loud voice he called to all the birds that fly directly overhead, 'Come, gather for the great supper of God, to eat the flesh of kings, the flesh of captains, the flesh of mighty men, the flesh of horses and their riders, and the flesh of all men, both free and slave, both small and great'" (Rev. 19:17–18 ESV). Moreover, we are told elsewhere that accompanying the Lamb to battle are the saints: "They will make war with the Lamb, but the Lamb will conquer them, because he is Lord of lords and King of kings, and those accompanying the Lamb are the called, chosen, and faithful" (Rev. 17:14). Therefore, these reasons show that the armies that follow Jesus into battle in Revelation 19:14 are most certainly saints, not angels. To be sure, this is not to say that angels will not also accompany Jesus into battle. They likely will, since executing his judgments is a role for angels. But in this particular verse, the armies refer to the redeemed saints.

17. *Paul and the Parousia: An Exegetical and Theological Investigation* (Peabody: Hendrickson, 1997), 82.

18. Matt. 11:12; 12:29; 13:19; John 6:15; 10:12, 28–29; Acts 8:39; 23:10; 2 Cor. 12:2, 4; 1 Thess. 4:17; Jude 1:23; Rev. 12:5.

19. For an expanded discussion of these four reasons, see *Antichrist Before the Day of the Lord*, 87–100.

20. For additional argumentation on the first reason, see *Antichrist Before the Day of the Lord*, 88–9.

21. For further argumentation that shows this group is the church and/or including all of God's people, see *Three Views on the Rapture: Pretribulation, Prewrath, or Posttribulation*, 2nd ed., ed. Alan Hultberg (Grand Rapids: Zondervan, 2010), 129–37.

22. Louw and Nida, *Greek-English Lexicon of the New Testament.*

23. For more discussion on this, see *Antichrist Before the Day of the Lord*, 159–61.

24. For debate on whether the particular harvest mentioned in Revelation 14:14–16 depicts the rapture or a judgment harvest, see *Three Views on the Rapture*, 134–5.

25. We could add a fifth prophetic event that must occur before the day of the Lord: the unbelieving world saying, "Peace and security!" In his first epistle to the Thessalonians, Paul taught that the world, oblivious to the impending wrath, will be uttering this slogan before the day of the Lord. "Now when they are saying, 'There is peace and security,' then sudden destruction comes on them, like labor pains on a pregnant woman, and they will surely not escape" (1 Thess. 5:3).

26. The core of prewrath teaching is attested in the first century by the earliest Christian document outside the New Testament called the *Didache*, "the Teaching" (a.k.a. *The Teaching of the Twelve Apostles*), pronounced DID-ah-kay. It is dated between A.D. 50–120. In addition to the *Didache*, there were seven subsequent early church documents and writers before A.D. 250 who all attest that the church will suffer during the Antichrist's persecution: *Epistle of Barnabas* (c. 80–c. 100), *Shepherd of Hermas* (c. 95–c. 150), Justin Martyr (c. 110–c. 165), Irenaeus (c. 120–c. 202), Tertullian (c. 145–c. 220), Hippolytus (c. 185–c. 235), and Cyprian (c. 200–c. 258). I have documented their actual statements in the appendix "What Did the Early Church Believe?" in *Antichrist Before the Day of the Lord*, 193–200.

Scripture Index

About the Author

Alan E. Kurschner is director of Eschatos Ministries, dedicated to teaching biblical eschatology from a futurist, premillennial, prewrath perspective. Kurschner holds an M.A. in biblical languages from Gordon-Conwell Theological Seminary.

For more resources, visit Eschatos Ministries:
www.AlanKurschner.com

BECAUSE JESUS WARNED:

"Remember, I have told you ahead of time." –Matt 24:25

ESCHATOS
PUBLISHING

www.AlanKurschner.com

information can be obtained
ICGtesting.com
the USA
1923231216
BV00002B/143/P